In The Key of C

The Life of Frank Mills

In The Key of C
The Life of Frank Mills

By
ELSIE ROSE

(an authorized biography)

MUSIC BOX DANCER
PUBLICATIONS LTD
Markham, Ontario
Canada

Canadian Cataloguing in Publication Data

Rose, Elsie, 1958 -
In The Key of C – The Life of Frank Mills

Includes bibliographical references and index.
ISBN 0-921965-42-7

1. Mills, Frank, 1942 - 2. Composers – Canada – Biography. 3. Pianists – Canada – Biography. I. Title.

ML417.M3R79 1998 781.64'092 C98-901325-1

Published by Music Box Dancer Publications Ltd.
2600 John Street, Unit 220
Markham, Ontario, Canada L3R 3E3
Phone (905) 475-1848 Fax (905) 474-9870

For Sybil, Larry, Marge
When all the words have been written,
your unconditional love endures forever

For Dennis, Nora, Cindy, Heather
for believing in me

To Life
The greatest gift we will ever receive

Author's Acknowledgments

Songs are like children. You give birth to them. You raise them. You send them out into the world and you hope that they'll be loved and prosper and do well. And you send a piece of yourself out there everytime. This book is of equal stature, effort and grace. It, too, is the song of a life. If this book encourages more people to appreciate Frank, to want to learn more about him, or to listen to his music, my job will have been done. Writing this book would not have been possible without the kind and willing assistance of many people who know and love Frank. Thank you, for your time, conversation and insights.

Carl Banas
Peter Batson
Liz Batson
Craig Bignell
Brian Edwards
Bill Girdwood
Michael Hoppe
Miles Jackson
Geoffrey Johnstone
Mark LaLama
Richard Lawton
John Loweth
Sandra Mills
Jonathan Mills
Nancy Mills
Hayward Parrott
Karen Rambeau
Kathy Stone

Special thanks to Bobbi Gray, former president of the Frank Mills Fan Club; Bernadette Couture, former vice-president of the Frank Mills Fan Club, and Fan Club members Janice Anderson, Joan Jefferess, Arlene Seitz, Judy Mills and Toni Stringam for your insights.

Thank you, Joyce Gariepy and H. Watson for your eagle-eye.

Frank, thank you for embarking on a work (a swampland) of your soul. It was, at times, like a gritty little mosquito-infested breeding hole on the back forty. Everything you have ever yearned for, learned, seen, thought, or dreamed was recorded on those tapes and emerged in this written form. Thank you for "shrinking" and pouring out your soul. I have been changed by exploring and being invited into that soul.

CONTENTS

PROLOGUE

Frantic to support his family, he obtained a City of Toronto cab driver's license, from Beck's Cabs, on March 22, 1978. Meanwhile, Frank was still working with Michael Hoppe. "For over a year we discussed Frank doing cover versions of existing hits like ABBA's 'Knowing Me, Knowing You,' and 'Dancing Queen.' He was arranging these various hits at his own cost. Unfortunately, after spending considerable time with him and trying to get this going, it didn't work out. I don't remember exactly why it didn't work. Maybe the arrangements weren't distinctive enough or the songs didn't have any style or something like that. At the time, much of the repertoire I was getting was from Europe, where famous instrumentalists made huge amounts of money doing cover versions of existing songs. We were trying to duplicate a successful formula. He was terribly disappointed. I told him we couldn't use the arrangements. He was at the end. I remember him telling me he was going to drive a cab. I said to him, 'I feel really bad about this. Do you have any other music I can put out?' He showed me the vocal record. 'Sorry, Chappy, we'll have to pass on that one.' 'Do you have anything else?' I asked again," remembers Michael Hoppe.

"I've got a tape in the drawer," Frank said.

"Bring it in, Chappy and we'll hav a listen," Hoppe responded. The next week, after listening to two or three pieces he said, "We've heard enough. We don't need to go through the entire album. What about your performance royalties for your best two cuts. Let's hear them."

"The best one is 'The Poet and I.' "

"A soft romantic ballad," Hoppe nodded after hearing the piece. "The other one?"

" 'Music Box Dancer.' "

"Hmmm, a little piano tinkly thing," Hoppe announced. "I tell you what, Chappy. We'll put out a disk jockey single with A side 'The Poet and I,' and B side that little tinkly thing, what you call, er, humn, hmmm ... 'Music Box Whatever.' "

"How many do you think you'll sell?" asked Frank.

"Who knows? Maybe two thousand, maybe five thousand, maybe seven thousand? There's really no way to tell," the director shrugged.

While there are neither pews, candles or organs among these giants, Frank's sugarbush is every bit a cathedral. There are twinges of something beyond awe, beauty and pleasure in this place of grace. The delicate drips in stereo as sap trickles into metal buckets, produces a holy echo that carries for amazing distances on crisp spring mornings. This wooded orchestra plays its balm for the heart – and soul.

"Plink, plink, plink."

"Plink, plink, plink."

"Two drops to the heartbeat," is an old sugarmaker's formula for a pulse-quickening flow. As the buckets fill with the nectar, the melody of plinks becomes deeper and richer.

"Plunk, plunk, plunk."

"Pluuunnnk, pluunnnk."

"Pluuuuuukkkk, pluuuuukkkkk, plunnnnnnnkkkkkk."

For Frank, the sea is yet another symphony, a moody lady, a mirror to all who confront her. Her numerous musical selections include: grandeur in a storm, glassy surface in a calm, the deep fathoms of her abysses, her quick vicissitudes, her direful deceptions. She carries manhood to die, to be transported, to seek adventure and to become rich. There is a key of sea for all these times, happy, melancholy, sad. They tell of noble events and sorrowful partings, of the dashing spray, of living by the sea, of grim accounts of wreckage as fishermen have gone out from inlets and little harbors to cast their nets. Sailors of the high seas feared to sing of the dangers of the sea. They preferred songs about the girls left on shore or the good times they would have when they got back again. Seafarer Frank, the man of diesel engines and generators, plotting and barometers, speaks about the sea as a navigable element and an intimate companion.

There are sea sanctuaries that captivate the senses, that tempt you to linger in their tranquillity and leave you feeling peaceful. After dark, the Bahamian stars take over. On a clear night, there is an overwhelming urge to lie on your back and stare up at the sparkling sky. For the briefest possible moment, in this mere splinter of time in the warm womb of the Bahamian sky, time seems to stand still.

The creative dilemma and the image problem have been ongoing sources of frustration for Frank. "It's hard to define me, an instrumental artist. To some people I'm dull and boring. There is this side of me that is creative. But there is also this side of me that is business-like. The cards I got were 50 percent music and 50 percent business. I've met many artistic, creative people who got about 98 percent music and about two percent business. They are the 'I'm dedicated to my ax (my music) kind of people.' "

In showbiz, that translates to nothing to talk about. "I'm a middle-aged, suburbia-type guy, who looks like somebody's father. That ain't gonna sell music videos. The media found it hard to grasp onto anything about me as a person. Bob Dylan? Look out. You don't know what he's going to do. He might take his clothes off. People who are successful with the press tend to have this kind of image. I'm just a normal guy. Some musicians I have met are so obsessed with music. All they know and talk about is music. It's them and "their ax." While music is a part of life, it's not all there is. Music is a small part of all the things I do to enjoy life. Life is my profession, music is my hobby."

1

Oatmeal Cookies and Eighty-Eight Keys

The delicious air, made potent with the fragrance of warm butterscotch oatmeal cookies, flowed like a balm through the Mills home. So sweet, the smell of safety. Elsie Mills cooked oatmeal for breakfast for her children Frankie and Kathy, insisted they retrieve wool mittens and socks from dresser drawers, and frequently baked the tasty treats. Their delectable aroma lingered over the petunias, freshly mowed lawn, and the peace and tranquillity of the Mills home in Mount Royal.

For Frank Mills, (the grown-up version of Frankie), a middle-aged salt, songwriter, sugarmaker, captain of his own yacht and grandfather named "Grumps," those home-baked morsels conjure happy times, family laughter, postwar affluence and innocent hope. While he's tried many concoctions for one of his favorite comfort foods, he's never been able to duplicate his mother's recipe. Butterscotch oatmeal cookies along with fishing, music, bicycles and model airplanes were the young Frankie's view of heaven.

Frankie's father, Frank Mills Sr. was a young dream chaser who eagerly burst on Canadian soil in 1920. Alone and undaunted, the 20-year-old candy maker left Canterbury, England, for adventure and opportunity in Canada. He ventured that the West might be a good place to start his candy business. After stoking wheat, plowing fields, tending to farm animals and fixing machinery on a wheat farm, he headed for better prospects in eastern Canada. For several years he lived in Verdun, a suburb of Montreal, and worked for Stillwell's Candies, the makers of English toffee. He declined an offer to buy the business. Impressed and enthusiastic about the new land, he sent glowing tributes back to his mother Mary Banning, father Robert Mills and siblings Hilda, Charles, Sidney, Alf and Robert (Bob). The family joined him several years later.

Frankie's mother, Elsie Ethel Mills (nee Burton), was one of nine children (Harry, Arthur (Joe), George, Bill, Frank, Catherine (Kitty), Hilda, Gladys), born to Catherine Macbeth and John Burton, a crane operator. Elsie Mills and her family came from England about 1912 and went to Kenora, Ontario. Rumor has it that the Kenora Archives have photographs of the family's trek of "seven children and a piano" (two children were born in Canada). Indians scared Catherine, Elsie's mother. When the cold, harsh and howling Canadian winters became unbearable, the family moved to Montreal where John got a job as a crane operator on the docks.

Frank Sr. met Aunt Hilda (his future sister-in-law) through work. They dated for about a year. Frankie's father realized he was in love with Elsie and married her shortly after. Part of the cash-only generation, they waited to have children until they could afford them. Kathleen (Kathy), their first child, was born in 1938 while the couple was living in Verdun, Montreal. When Frank Sr. was 40, their second child and only son, Frank William, arrived on June 27, 1942 (they called him Frankie). Frankie spent his first four years in the Montreal community of Notre Dame de Grace. When he was five years old, the family moved to Mount Royal, another community in Montreal.

From almost anywhere in Montreal you can see Mont Real – or as Montrealers call it, *la montagne* (the mountain) as it looms up in the middle of the city like a natural obelisk. As Frankie recalls, when his father arrived in Montreal he kissed the large wooden, weather-beaten cross at the top of Mont Real. He also carved his initials in the monument's base. The illuminated steel cross that now stands at the top of the peak commemorates a wooden one raised in 1643 after the community's deliverance from a flood.

By the early 19th century, Montreal was Canada's premier city. Settlers passed through here, great ports were built, industry flourished, railroads were established and commerce was developed. Frankie's parents were afloat on a burgeoning postwar wave of prosperity. Canada was growing and discovering new industries and resources: the St. Lawrence Seaway, the Trans-Canada Highway, the Toronto subway, an ocean of oil in Alberta, aluminum at Kitimat, British Columbia, nickel at Thompson, Manitoba.

The dust bowl Depression had dashed the hopes of many Canadians. In the Second World War, Canadian soldiers and war workers, unable to grasp or care about such concepts as democracy and humanitarian efforts, fought for "Home." With its friends, family, daily activities, and emotional significance, "Home" was worth the battle. Advertising, fiction, magazine articles, poems and newspaper stories recreated the warm and cozy vision. Family members embraced returning soldiers in Coca-Cola ads, and "Home loving, Home owning craftsmen" built cars. Songs such as 'Sentimental Journey,' 'Don't Sit Under the Apple Tree,' and 'I'll be Seeing You,' appealed to the desire for reunion and the return of loved ones. After years of deprivation, poverty and desperate need, new immigrants gasped at produce and meat-filled stalls at the markets. The real estate market was booming. New arrivals and rural people moved to the borderland between city and country. Homeownership in the "suburbs" was the symbol of the successful, young postwar family.

Canada's new love of mobility also fueled the growth of the suburbs. By 1945, automobile ownership, symbolizing the good life, technology, luxury and freedom of movement, ranked second in the minds of Canadians. Advertisements hailed the virtues of hydro-glide transmissions, flashy, glistening chrome, swept-fin styling and a new and better model every October. Car names such as Strato-Chief and Rocket '88 symbolized technology while Bel Air and Parisienne evoked luxury. Chevrolet ads, with a picture of parents and two children cruising along an open road, hailed the message, "Give Your Family Big Car Dependability."

Tires were needed to run those automobiles. It was a fortuitous time, financially speaking, for Frank Sr., an ambitious, spirited entrepreneur. Frank Sr. acquired a partnership in a tire shop at 164 Gallery Square, a few minutes walk from downtown Montreal. He bought out the partner and turned the business into the thriving and prosperous Mills Tire Service. His wife did the accounting and handled the office while he managed the staff, entertained his clients and sought new business. While he served the growing residential market, much of his success came in providing tires and service to commercial clients.

In that era, whether it was a coal miner's humble dwelling or a millionaire's mansion, a house was not a home without a piano. In the Mills home, the small upright Heinzman held a place of honor in the living room. It was the complete instrument, with the power to evoke the illusion of a singer, a French horn, a flute, a cello – it was like a one-man orchestra. Frankie and his sister Kathy arrived home from school to hear their mother playing the classics or tunes of the day. The sound of the piano was full, pleasurable and always present in the Mills home.

Friday and Saturday evenings were full of laughter, hoards of people, piano playing, sing-a-longs, and tables laden with food. Kathy says of her entrepreneur, outgoing father, "He always wanted lots of people around. He was a real party animal. I remember his love of music and beautiful voice. We gathered around the Heinzman. Dad sang and Mom played the piano." An Irish tenor, Frank Sr. rendered his favorite tunes including 'The Rose of Tralee,' 'Galway Bay,' 'Molly Malone,' 'Danny Boy,' 'When Irish Eyes are Smiling,' 'Tipperary,' and 'I'll Take you Home Again, Kathleen' (from which Frankie's sister got her name). Sensitive and emotional, Frank Sr. frequently burst into tears while singing the old-country songs. "Mother cooked and cooked and cooked. We always had many guests," remembers Kathy. "Lots of them were business associates. Dad always looked after his clients."

To Frankie, the piano was never a mystery. It was a friend and constant companion. Early in his life, Frankie felt the stirrings of musical feeling. "I was about three, and I remember fiddling with the piano. It was in me. It wasn't banging around, making noise, like some small children do. I sat down to play it. They told me I wrote a little song called 'Bird on Fence.' The spark of music was awakened in me at an early age. This was not a curiosity about the mechanism, it was the music. I felt it," reflects Frankie.

When the family moved to Mount Royal, Frankie's musical interests flourished. Frankie spent hours composing tunes on the keyboard. He had learned to pick out melodies from listening to his father sing and his mother play the instrument. Linking notes into melodies, he played the pieces over and over. Many of the tunes were his own inventions. He only quit playing when his fingers were tired. For this young boy, the sounds were reassuring, and created a reality that was soothing and peaceful. The infinite possibilities of the piano's eighty-eight keys held him spellbound. He enjoyed catching the waves and riding them. The sound wrapped him in a protective cloak. On the eighty-eight keys he could express himself and release the creative energy that bubbled inside his young heart.

His sister Kathy remembers, "When Frankie was about four or five years old, he played songs on the piano – from memory – without having a lesson. I was around eight or 10 years old at the time. I had spent weeks practicing my piano lessons. Then Frankie played the songs I had just played. It was frustrating. So I quit. I couldn't compete. Mother never had to get him to practice. Frankie did it himself." Kathy remembers her brother's great joy at making up songs, "It came out of his head. Frequently, after waking up in the morning he said, 'I just wrote a song.' Then he played it. For as long as I can remember he wrote songs." At around seven years old, the young boy took piano lessons. Frankie adored his piano teacher, Mr. Lewis, almost as much as the music. Mr. Lewis asked his pupil if he wanted to be a concert pianist. Frankie said he didn't think so.

The Mills home at 169 Chester Avenue, about halfway on the long street, was a two-storey, grey and red brick building. It had a steep roof and a high Gothic porch rising over the entrance doorway. The new home's main feature was a picture window which defined the front of the house and dominated the living room. It was every postwar's family dream to have such a tidy, little home complete with picture window, wall-to-wall carpet, garden, and a "barbecue" in the backyard. In affluent Mount Royal, a young community of upper-class immigrants, odors of burnt meat frequently wafted between neighbors' yards. Sprinklers were also turned on to perform their hypnotic fan dance across the carefully sculptured lawns.

Canada's national icon, the sugar maple, also the official tree of Vermont, lined both sides of the street. The maples in Frankie's first sugarbush (a grove of sugar maple trees, also called sugar grove, sugar orchard and sugar woods) rose tall and straight, producing clear, perfect boles without side branches for a considerable height. In the summer, the maples spun their double-winged seeds, the color of bones, sluggishly in the sweltering air. The large, full crown and branches were low enough to climb. Frankie marveled at the four-season display, particularly the fall pallet of reds, oranges, yellows, or combination of all three. Elsie frequently found her son lying in a pile of autumn leaves, an expression of pure bliss on his face. In autumn, the lush green foliage on Chester Avenue burst into a magnificent display of crimson and gold fireworks that slowly faded to lifeless brown and grey.

On Saturday night, Elsie served her son dinner in the playroom in the basement. "Maybe that fostered the loner in me," says Frankie of his boyhood. "Saturday night was always a big treat. Eating in front of the television.

Mom made dinner for me. I'd enjoy eating her great cooking at one of those maple veneer TV tables, a precarious little tray on folding legs. Kathy was off somewhere. She was four years older so we didn't play together. I spent many Saturday nights alone." For a special treat, his mother ordered St. Hubert chicken, about $1.20 at the time. It was the latest "in" thing to have food delivered to your door. For Frankie, a St. Hubert television commercial is a cherished childhood memory. "A yellow Volkswagen with a red rooster on top dashed across the television screen, to the sound of 'Cluck Cluck Cluck. Here's All You Do. Cluck Cluck Cluck. St. Hubert Barbecue.' "

Frankie joined the ranks of millions of Canadians meeting the one-eyed monster. Throughout the nation, people flocked to living rooms, schools, hospitals and places of business to gawk at the 19-inch world, a tiny screen embedded in a large wooden case. Only the automobile outranked the arrival of the television, one of the most significant technological innovations of the twentieth century. An entire country was bewitched by the black and white picture flickering before them. You were envied if you had the first TV on the block.

Frankie's imagination had previously been entertained by the radio programs *The Lone Ranger*, *The Green Hornet*, and *The Adventures of Superman*. Before television, the radio sat in the living room along with the Heinzman piano. He learned the lyrics of the popular songs and tried to guess the right answers along with the game show contestants. Frankie played records on the record player, an awkward, prone-to-breakdown contraption that usually played the scratched records at the wrong speed.

He grew up watching the long-running television shows *Gunsmoke* (1955-75), *Superman* (1951 - 57), *Rin Tin Tin* (1954 - 59), *Bonanza* (1959 - 73), and *Ed Sullivan* (1948 - 71). Television brought the world of new appliances, entertainment and convenience to wondering eyes in the fifties. Companies created countless labor-saving devices: electric stoves; vacuum cleaners; electric refrigerators; toasters; air conditioners. Young wives in pedal pushers and tube tops were expected to cook and clean. Meanwhile, the men slayed corporate dragons. "Unfortunately, a postwar "good" Mom rewarded her kids with food. That wasn't good for me," remembers Frankie. Some of his favorite dishes were roast beef and Yorkshire pudding, pumpkin pie, lemon tarts, pineapple upside-down cake and butterscotch oatmeal cookies. Frankie's mother baked for the ladies who gathered each week in the living room. "Mother was a member of the church guild and bridge club. Eight or ten ladies met at our house on Wednesday night. I'd eat the cookies and date squares. Mom always made more because she knew I would eat half of them." When she wasn't cooking or attending to matters at Mills Tire Service, she read. "We used to say, 'oh God, Mom's got her nose in a book. We won't see her for a week.' "

The tire store was booming, money was abundant and Frankie and Kathy never wanted for anything. "Christmas was Dad's gift to everybody. There were presents galore, the fire was going, and it was everything a Canadian Christmas should be."

The outlook reported by *Canadian Business* was "Getting places, reaching for the top, stepping on the gas and at all costs keep going." Dads worked hard to achieve success, pay for the newly acquired homes, washers, slabs of frozen beef, and modern appliances. Dining with Mom and Dad was a ritual, a tradition. At around six p.m., families brooded, fretted and longingly gazed out the living room window for Dad's arrival. The corner office demons frequently held him hostage. In 1956 the *Post* dubbed this growing work ethic and its devastating consequences, "executive fatigue." Today, we know it as "stress."

Drop-dead eating habits contributed to the problem. Unaware of the benefits of low-fat, high-fibre diets, the postwar generation fried, boiled, cooked and baked their way to coronary heart disease. Mothers boiled the nutrients out of potatoes, cabbage, and other vegetables. Every kitchen had stable items of milk, meat and potatoes. Home entertaining was fun, cheap and part of the social fabric. Booze was a social habit if handled with moderation. "New product promotions (in the fifties) convinced homemakers that the ultimate in culinary chic was producing four-layer cakes covered with fluffy frosting mix; glazing Klik or Prem with pineapple and calling it 'Hawaiian'; topping sweet potatoes with marshmallows and adding canned soup to every casserole," write Margaret Fraser and Carol Ferguson in *A Century of Canadian Home Cooking*.

This "working man" attitude likely contributed to Frank Sr.'s life-long battle with heart disease and high blood pressure. Frankie grew up seeing a pill-popping, doctor-visiting, tired father. "I don't ever remember him being well. He was always taking pills and seeing the doctor. He came home for naps every afternoon because he was so tired. They didn't know anything at the time, but his health was a disaster," recounts Frankie.

When Frankie was five years old, his father had a major heart attack and was admitted to the Montreal Jewish Hospital on Cotes des Neiges Street. Not allowed to visit, the young boy waved to his Dad from the sidewalk below. For someone who wasn't expected to return home, Frank Sr. made a remarkable recovery.

Massive construction in the suburbs meant most pupils spent at least a part of their elementary years in a new building. With Carlyle School still under construction, Frankie attended kindergarten in the Mount Royal Recreation Centre.

He attended grades one through seven at Carlyle School, within walking distance of his home on Chester Avenue. Like houses, elementary schools reflected the modernism of the age. The architects who designed the cozy homes designed the schools. Carlyle School, a two-storey affair, had a flat roof and many windows. A concrete-pillar entrance accented the red brick building. Inside, new classrooms were finished in light colors, pastel with a dull gloss paint and green blackboards. Modern linoleum was the floor covering of choice. The desks were light-colored Formica-topped and unblemished by pens, scratches or knife carvings of previous pupils. The classroom smelled of chalk dust, warm brown apple cores, the droopy remains of bologna crescents, peanut butter and jelly crusts, and lead pencil shavings that crammed the black metal waste basket. Frankie loved playing with his friends in the playground filled with the latest slides and swings. He kept his desk immaculate, meticulously cleaning any eraser residue or crayon marks after completing his lessons.

A Raleigh three-speed racing bike was Frankie's chief mode of transportation during these years. "I loved my bike. It was the neatest thing. It had a banana seat, saddle bag and Dynamo spotlight that ran on the tire and made its own electricity. I used to take my bike out at night just to see the lights light up." When he was about 10 years old, the ever-curious inventor Frankie tried to put chains on his bicycle tires. He fell off, broke his leg and hobbled around on crutches for several months.

Despite the occasional accident, tinkering was an important part of Frankie's world. He always took things apart. He'd repeat the task until the left over pieces were correctly placed. When his Dad bought him a workbench, tinkering and building became even more of an obsession. He spent long hours in the basement, re-engineering clocks, toasters, lamps and tools, building model airplanes and cars, and unintentionally inhaling model glue. Somewhat tipsy, he slept off the adhesive's effects and returned to the nearby park to fly his aircraft.

The organized and meticulous Frankie insisted his toys be immaculate and lined up in perfectly straight rows. He frequently washed his toys, seldom letting other kids play with his tractor and trailer set or model train set. "I didn't want anybody to mess them up. They had to be just right." This stance, however, wasn't play. He discovered that letting his toys get bumps, scratches and scars was a lot more fun.

Mostly, his vivid imagination entertained him. "I didn't have to go very far. I didn't need anybody else to play with. I made it up myself." He faithfully read *Mother West Wind's Children* (written by Thornton W. Burgess) published in the *Montreal Daily Star*. Young readers learned about the lives of wild neighbors and learned much, quite unwittingly, about human traits such as curiosity, kindness, thrift, courage and wisdom. In the stories Reddy Fox and Billy Mink are mischief makers. Shadow the Weasel is sly and cruel. Little Joe Otter and Jerry Muskrat are slow travelers. Reddy Fox never catches Peter Rabbit. He is forever trying to steal chickens and eggs from Farmer Brown. Characters played out stories such as 'Danny Meadow Mouse Learns Why his Tail Is Short,' 'Why Peter Rabbit's Ears are Long,' and 'Mr. Toad's Old Suit,' on the green meadows, at the smiling pool and the laughing brook. Watching the antics of these critters, Frankie imagined his own meadow with trees, hills, valleys and a "real" tractor in the field.

This curious and likable kid had a solemn and volatile side. He earned the nickname "The Judge" for his serious behavior. Even at a young age handling fatigue was difficult. When his mother woke him up early for his afternoon surprise birthday party, the tired and annoyed Frankie blurted, "I'm not going to a pig's party." He apologized, joined the party and slept more than usual after the guests went home. "Feisty little Frankie was a terror. He was very demanding in what he wanted if he didn't get his own way," recalls Frankie. Perhaps it was the start of Frankie's sense of himself as strong and reliant. The occasional outbursts likely helped develop his ruthless determination.

The silver screen was fodder for Frankie's growing imagination. Saturday afternoons the Mount Royal Theatre, with its vaulted ceilings and large screen, was packed with kids totally absorbed in the compressed, high-velocity emotional dramas unfolding before them. Frankie watched pirates raid ocean vessels, clowning thugs get the girl, scoundrels rob banks, cynical servants comment on the shenanigans of the principals, over-the-hill prize

Frank's View

Does a Child Have Musical Talent?

It's difficult to say whether a child has talent. Capacity can be viewed as a line that ranges from little talent on one end to genius on the other. Looking at musical ability this way, each person has talent, but some children have more than others. Young children naturally respond to sound without necessarily having any musical ability. They will often sing in tune, ask for pieces to be played, pick out songs on the piano, radio or other instrument. They may sway, move and bounce rhythmically to melody. They are often affected by changes in sound, talk about music and ask questions about music. These might be good clues to determine whether a child is interested in music. They may not.

Certainly, if these indicators are there, it's a good idea to gently foster the interest. Talent also depends on a great many factors including a music-friendly atmosphere, the child's temperament, supportive family and teachers, friends who share the interest, persistence, luck, determination and creativity.

Generally speaking, children who express some musical talent will have evidence of a musical ear, sensitivity, coordination and musical intuition in varying degrees in the following areas:

* *Ability to discern pitch.* Being able to determine quality of sound, the degree of acuteness or graveness of tones. Singing in tune, matching high or low pitches. Remembering melodies.
* *Ability to discern rhythm.* Keeping time, repeating rhythms and combining these skills. Sensing changes of speed and tempo.
* *Ability to discern timbre.* Discriminating sounds made by each instrument. Sensing disturbances within specific instrument ranges.
* *Sensitivity to music.* Ability to discriminate between phrasing and ways of making sounds. Sensitivity to loud and soft changes.
* *Psychomotor skill.* Hand-eye coordination, strength and agility to play a specific musical instrument.
* *Desire to perform.* The child takes pleasure in playing, singing and performing for other people.

These are not hard and fast rules. Many musicians lack skills in certain areas but compensate for it in other areas. A good music education can help a child develop the stronger and weaker parts of their ability.

Personality

Certain personality traits, in varying degrees, may be helpful to sustain and influence the child through years of study, practice and performing:

* *Determination.* For some children, music is a need and a drive rather than a pastime or hobby. They display high enthusiasm for a particular instrument.
* *Inner motivation.* Creativity and ingenuity are strong personality traits in reaching a goal. The child may be absorbed while playing or practicing. Succeeding, winning and performing are important.
* *Persistence and self-discipline.* The child is able and willing to work for his goals.
* *Originality.* Creativity, risk-taking, problem-solving and intuitive acting may be present in varying degrees.

The hunger for exploration and variation, however, may produce frustrations. While a child may be a quick learner, a problem solver, and an independent thinker, there is a downside. He may be a careless learner, have tunnel vision, overfantasize, complicate matters, fret and try to overachieve, be stubborn or determined. The child must learn to maintain a tolerable balance between forces that drive him internally and the determination and persistence required to master musical skills and language.

On the other hand, a child who doesn't possess these personality traits may do equally well. He may go for many years, without working or playing at anything. Thereafter, he may have to make the effort and develop the discipline to advance further. Deciding to do something may fuel the ambition.

It is difficult to tell what musical talents will show themselves, or to predict how great the potential is or how far a talent will go. Talent aside, musical creativity should be encouraged in everyone. While everyone is not born with or can aspire to musical greatness, music, in its many forms, enhances and enriches our lives. You don't need to be a Mozart to enjoy or play the gift of music.

Frank Mills

fighters make a comeback, harridans and shrews get revenge and mad scientists invent creatures in their laboratories.

While he enjoyed the cast of gangsters, cops, animals, Moms and Dads, armies, thieves, lovers, kings, detectives and priests, he was fascinated by the sound of the orchestrated chaos: engines roaring; tires squealing; wind screaming; men groaning; bodies thumping; footsteps creaking; clothes rustling; violins screeching. He was particularly drawn to the music score, frequently a symphony sequence, as each scene built up the level of suspense and anxiety. Rhapsodic strings accompanied a love scene. Ominous music introduced a train wreck. Light music presented a fashion show or the capering of animals in a zoo.

The Western, with its gunfight, fistfight, chase on horseback, saloon girl and lonely landscape, was his favorite movie. The hero crawled across deserts on his hands and knees, climbed rock faces in the blinding sun, starved in a snowbound cabin in the mountains, walked or rode for miles on end with near mortal wounds, survived for days without water, shelter or sleep. The hero exercised self-discipline, determination, knowledge, skill, ingenuity, and judgment in the face of overwhelming odds. Fiction, no doubt, but nourishment for a growing boy. The hero's ideas matched his own.

Most importantly, Westerns were Frankie's first fling with the classics. "A fiery horse with the speed of light, a cloud of dust and a hearty Hi-Ho Silver! The Lone Ranger!" The stirring strains of a symphony accompanied these words. The opening is a close-up of a big white horse, ridden at a gallop by a masked avenger. The words "THE LONE RANGER" cover the image, to the sounds of *bang, bang*. The camera pulls back. The Lone Ranger and Silver gallop down into a sage-dotted valley, draw up momentarily in front of a butte, wheel, then take off again, Silver's white mane and tail waving in the wind. Frankie thought this music was written for the movie. In fact, the 17th century Italian composer Rossini wrote the movie's theme, the *William Tell* overture, while he was fishing, had his feet in the water discussing finance with a friend.

While other kids played sports – football, baseball, soccer, hockey, tennis, golf – the eighty-eight piano keys and other outdoor pursuits had a stronger pull for Frankie. "I'd see my friends playing soccer in the street. I'd be playing the piano. By my own choice. It was a release for me, even then. Perhaps it was childhood tensions. There was a lot of emotion involved in this. That continued until I quit piano and took up the trombone in grade seven," adds Frankie.

The Mills family spent many weekends fishing, enjoying the outdoors and entertaining Frank Sr.'s clients at the family cottage in Rosemere about a half hour drive from Montreal. During summer holidays the family lived at the cottage and Frank Sr. made a weekday commute to work. The cottage was the site of the usual hospitality – music, singing, food, drinks, chatter, laughter. One had to meander around the dusty records of the family's life – old heaters, outgrown shoes, worn clothing, furniture – to get at the piano hidden in the back of the garage. Frankie played songs from *Showboat*, pop music of the era and tunes he'd heard on the radio. To his surprise, delighted neighbors seated in lawn chairs, clapped enthusiastically when he opened the garage doors. "That was the first time I realized people liked my music. It was a shock. It took me a long time to get used to that idea. I didn't think anything more of it than me just having fun. That's probably where my entertainer roots started. Slowly but surely the kid's life was being directed to music, without me even knowing it."

Frankie enjoyed the visits to Uncle Bob's ranch about 30 miles up the St. Lawrence River from the family cottage. Uncle Bob, a friend from the tire business, raised race horses and black Belgians. It was a real treat when Frankie's father brought along a bucket of St. Hubert chicken.

At Rosemere, it was common to see a garter snake coiled blissfully in the sun or hear a big bullfrog croaking, his long thin red tongue flicking out for flies. Queen Anne's lace, yellow wildflowers, water lilies and wild brown brambles grew along the marshes beside the water's edge. During the day, the color of the water alternated between emerald green, cobalt blue, gold and copper. At dusk, the splashing waterfalls babbled like musical instruments.

Family fishing trips usually ended having caught half a dozen trout. In Frankie's eyes, his fisherman father, in his old straw hat, coveralls, rubber boots, who enjoyed those fishing excursions was a different man from the somber, driven, hard-working businessman at Mills Tire Service. Perhaps Frank Sr. was following his own dreams, looking for the fabled fish that got away. It was also part of Frank Sr.'s dilemma that later haunted him.

"Boiling" was part of the fun. Frankie had several fireplaces in the woods where he and some friends boiled potatoes and corn. The young boys later discovered that the golden cobs they had stolen from the neighboring farms was cattle corn. "It didn't matter. I was doing this for fun. It wasn't about eating. It was about the fire, boiling, preparation." Hiking, duck hunting, trapping animals and catching fish was really an excuse to cook pancakes on an open fire outdoors.

Birds and squirrels and mice and raccoons lived in the tall willows that dipped their roots into the waters along the banks of the Milles Illes River. Gentle currents swept around boulders and past their roots. Maples also created some of Frankie's perfect fishing places. Sunlight barely filtered through their huge crowns that cast giant shadows on the bank. One of his pockets was stuffed with a sandwich. The other pocket held worms and smelled of the dark backyard earth from where he dug the creatures. He spiked a worm on his small hook. He grabbed the rod and tossed the line into the water. The barb rolled to the pebbled bottom and sank under the brown, cool current. He waited. Nothing happened. He reeled in, tossed the line and tried again. After several tries he felt a tug on the line. The line tightened, the rod bent and a 10-inch trout with a fat belly splashed and rolled to the surface. This was it! He looked at the trout. The glassy eyes stared back, trying to tell him something. Frankie has been listening to that message ever since.

Throughout his youth, Frankie had numerous such spots along the river bank. He crawled through alders and thickets to get to one location, crossed waterfalls to get to another or jumped boulders and logs to get to one more. Discovering favorite fishing spots fostered his spirit of self-reliance that would carry him through many difficult years ahead. Fishing would become a lifelong passion, as the blood in his veins was replaced with the strong flow of the river. Some people assume fishing is an occupation for slow-witted ruminants. But fishing is more than tossing a worm or fly into the water and waiting for a fish to bite. Anglers are drawn to fishing in its many forms for its testing of self-reliance, coordination, strength and skill. The quarry is a cold-blooded creature near the bottom of the evolutionary scale. The angler's only chance of outwitting these denizens of the deep, with their quicksilver reflexes is to make himself inconspicuous – by placing himself into the natural environment, by keeping the sun on his face, hiding behind shrubs, trees and bushes, and creeping through the undergrowth.

Fish don't beep, whistle, squawk or hiss. Their dumbness is both a curse and a blessing. Any angler knows that casting your fly to a rising trout or watching your float intently for the slightest hint of a nibble is not for the faint-hearted. Your mind is focused. You can't worry about anything else. With the odds so high, why do people bother? If you are an angler – like Frankie – you know: it has to be difficult. The kill is uneventful: a creature of flashing silver is reduced to an inert, dead thing with dark and glutinous skin. Rather, it is the chase, the challenge, and the adventure which gives such pleasure.

Unknowingly, anglers talk of the poetics of fishing. They speak of the way the water floods the area, tree stumps, how a fish moves from its lay and rises for a fly, the smell of morning dew. Like surf and wind, a river's rush is one of the elemental and pure voices in which nature speaks. It is also one of Frankie's first symphonies. Waves crashing against the shore. The drumming, happy sound of water falling over a weir or small dam. The light, percussive effect of pebble hitting pebble. The brassy fanfare of spray against rock. The reedy drone of sand washing against a bar. The *plop* of beavers dropping into pools. Sandpipers calling *twee-wee-wee* as they fly over the water. In the fall, when the air is crisp and the leaves are coated with frost, the maples turn bright yellow, gold and red, and the swishing of leaf against leaf sounds like the rustle of a stiff taffeta gown. The books *A River Runs Through it*, *Big Two-Hearted River*, and *Fly Fishing Through the Mid-life Crisis* proclaim the sport's soulful and spiritual side. Fishing is really about the relationship between man and his environment, families, history, memory, innocence and peace.

Frankie spent many restless nights at the cottage chasing dreams. As the evening grew still, there was only the sound of the water trickling over rocks and through the sweep of fallen branches. The wind whistled off the calm waters. Frankie dreamed of becoming a fisherman and knowing the sea. As the sunlight cooled and the shadows lengthened moment by moment, he dreamed of his own, far-off place of peace.

Despite the music, fishing, the cottage, the affluence and Frankie's growing, vivid imagination, nurturing moments were rare in the Mills family. The occasions between men and women were never discussed. "We were the typical English immigrant family. There wasn't a lot of touching and affection. 'You didn't do it in England so you didn't do it here.' You kept a stiff upper lip. As a child, I didn't get much affection. To me, however, my parents seemed to be happily married. The only passion I saw was the quick kiss Dad gave Mom as he was leaving for work in the morning."

Frankie relished his getting-ready-for-bed routine. Sometimes, Frankie's father embraced his son as he drifted off to the stories and magic of *The Lone Ranger*, *Johnny Dollar* and *Groucho Marx* on the radio. These rare affectionate moments paled to the ambition and determination of a success driven philosophy. Frank Sr. wasn't a kids' dad. While he bought his son the best set of Lionel trains, he rarely played with him. Yet, he'd be the first to boast of his son's musical accomplishments.

Frankie remembers there being a bit of the "children should be seen and not heard" philosophy. He says his British born, devout Anglican parents were "so square." He wasn't supposed to spill the milk and mess up his clothes. He was to be the "perfect little kid." In some ways, Frankie feels he wasn't allowed to be a kid because of his parents' conservative, rigid approach to life and raising children. "I later learned that I was a well-behaved kid. I don't think I gave my parents or other kids many hassles. I thought all the other kids were like me. You didn't do anything wrong."

Attending St. Peter's Anglican Church was part of the "British" tradition. Frankie attended Sunday school, sang in the children's choir, executed each step of the altar boy ritual without a single mistake and sang in the adult choir when he was older. Those who arrived at church early, watched the others. Those who kneeled with their faces buried in their hands never looked up. The proud and the humble, all dressed in their best clothes gathered on Sundays and throughout the week at this centre of the community around the corner from the Mills home.

As far as young Frankie knew, he wanted to grow up and be a civil engineer. Not because he knew what they did. He liked the sound of the title and thought it might be something good. He considered medicine because doctors were revered. To this young boy, physicians were 'Gods.'

Frankie had a difficult time with one of his teachers at Carlyle School. She constantly tried to pull out the hairs on her chin. She petrified him with her frequent angry outbursts. Frank Sr. persuaded his son to continue. Frankie concluded good marks could avoid conflict with this temperamental, shaggy educator. Ironically, out of fear came brilliance. Frankie's academic achievement earned him a scholarship into high school.

He was, however, miffed when Frank Sr. gave Kathy $200 for her academic scholarship to high school. Frankie did not get anything. He was also disappointed that he never got a motorboat promised by his father. "In hindsight I suppose I was too young to have one. Maybe that's why I didn't get it. But these were two disappointments and they were important to me."

In grade seven Frankie took up the trombone. Quickly mastering the sacbut (a Moorish nickname), he played a trombone solo at the grade seven graduation ceremonies. Parents and kids packed the gymnasium for the event. His gift of playing by ear avoided embarrassment. Frankie, dressed in a blue blazer and blue pants, played the piece by ear. The temperature had soared, steaming up his glasses so the notes were unreadable. His beaming father was oblivious to his son's trumpet solo that sounded like a dying cow.

Life was simple for Frankie growing up in the '50s in Montreal. Like the maples that lined Chester Avenue, his grade school years bespoke honesty, dignity, and permanence. Mom's oatmeal butterscotch cookies, movies, television and outdoor activities at the family cottage were the stuff of boyhood dreams. "It was like heaven. It was a very secure time. Home was permanent and Dad was doing well. I was having fun with music. Mom was solid. We didn't know anything was wrong with her. You couldn't ask for anything better," remembers Frankie.

But even heaven has the haunting presence of death.

2

The Voice of an Anguished Soul

Death is a clever companion. It slithers in, so silently, so softly. Such gentleness being a paradox to the lingering sadness and terrible complexities it leaves behind. It tarried when Frank Sr. survived his first heart attack. But thoughts ran too deep for tears on that day, the sky the color of an angry bruise, when Frank Sr. told his son the sad news. "Mother has had some tests. She has to go into the hospital for surgery," his father told him about a year before he entered high school.

Although her condition was grave – she was slowly dying from cancer of the bladder, cervix and uterus – life seemed pretty normal. "Maybe I refused to believe it, or didn't want to believe it because Mom didn't look any different." Entering grade eight at Mount Royal High School, Frankie did all the things typical of a postwar generation teenager. He assumed his regular, responsible face to greet the world. His exterior was sunny despite the brewing storm.

Parents hoped to instill a "work hard, you have to make it" attitude in their children. Frankie likens this attitude to the 1989 film *Dead Poet's*

Society. In the movie, Robin Williams stars as an idealistic English teacher who tries to inspire a group of boys in a 1950s prep school to pursue individuality and creative endeavor, resulting in clashes with school and authorities. When one boy can't cope, he commits suicide. Frankie remembers several friends doing the same because they couldn't stand the pressure. "They just couldn't take the stress. It was too much." He himself didn't feel the burden because he was doing all the "be a success, do good work, be your best" things anyway. For him, high school was a "marvelous time, despite family difficulties."

He played trombone in the senior band, sang in the glee club, was part of the student council executive, the ski club and the camera club. A gender rotation policy prevented him from becoming student council president. It was a girl's turn the year he wanted to run for the position. "Captain of the team. That's the story of my life. For as long as I can remember it was always me who assumed or was put into a position of responsibility. Not that I minded. I liked being in control."

There was some unexpected upheaval when a group of tough-looking, immigrant children from Park Extension, another municipality, were bussed to the school. "We were the Goody-Two-Shoes, kids from the perfect, white Anglo Saxon homes. They were a different breed. This didn't sit well with many people. It was like bussing in Negroes in the '60s. This wasn't supposed to happen. There was an uproar when the kids from Park Extension arrived (Frankie and his friends (the Townies), called it Park Ex.) It was good for us. It mixed up the pot. There was funny little Millsie, the "townie," duckied up in his gussy clothes. The other guys were smoking, talking rough and looking cool in their jeans. But it turned out okay. Later, I played in a rock band with Joe Padulo, a guy from Park Ex."

The gregarious side of Frankie took great pride in organizing ski trips, photography shows and student council meetings. Every Saturday, the parking lot of Mount Royal High School was jammed with eight buses loaded with kids enroute to a ski trip. Frankie was the lead singer at the back of the bus. He also managed the $800.00 weekly revenue the ski club earned from these recreational trips.

He was especially fond of his music activities. Each fall he participated in writing and performing songs for the school's Christmas show. Dr. Harrison Jones, the high school music teacher, waved a baton and in return obtained the best in musical skill from the bands, choirs and instrumental choirs. Frankie frequently played solo numbers at band performances. He led the trumpet "Charge" cheer at the intercollegiate hockey games. Richard Lawton, later dean of music at McGill University in Montreal, was in grade nine when Frankie was in grade eleven. Lawton remembers him as being friendly, outgoing, a very popular fellow, a good trombone player and pianist.

While Kathy remembers her brother being busy with numerous activities, she enjoyed dinners together. "He was gone all the time. He was doing his piano, his clubs, his music. But we were always together for dinner." Kitchen duty was more than washing dishes. "We danced. Frankie sang to a song he'd made up. The dishtowel and plate was in his hand as he spun around. We'd laugh and joke. It was so much fun," reflects Kathy.

Inspired by his English teacher, Dr. Buchanan, Frankie began to write poetry. Dr. Buchanan usually diverted from the prescribed English program and taught his own style English course. He guided, encouraged and inspired his students to study Shakespeare, Keats, Wordsworth, Shelley, Byron and Melville. He taught with a wry passion and made the words catch fire. "He had this wonderful way of stimulating young people to think about Shakespeare. He was an inspiration. Those lines and lines of poetry we learned have served me well throughout my life," says Frankie. It was also Buchanan who joked when his student got a music scholarship. "He laughed and said; 'Oh, my God, Mills. There you are, a paradox. A music scholarship.' " Buchanan found it ironic that someone who played the trombone and did musical things was also good in English. Frankie's 8B Guidance Exercise book documents his early poetic works.

Retain your faith young heart
by Frank Mills

"Retain your faith young heart"
Hath said an aged man to me.
For somehow God hath given life and strife
To comfort thee.

Just as the world that fights each man
Who gives his very soul to seek

Why fellow men do criticize
And cause beloved ones to weep.

"But hark!" he said, make no amends
That they are other than great friends
And question not but what they do
For God doth run their living too.

Tis often that the road's worst bend
Doth prove most scenic in the end.

Grief and lingering, pathetic sadness played an important role in shaping Frankie's high school years as he watched his mother, a robust, healthy woman turn into a resemblance of a Hiroshima survivor. At the time, the medical profession didn't know much about treating cancer. She was badly burnt by cancer treatments. In the first operation, the lower bowel was removed. "She had a bag here and a bag there. It was awful," remembers Frankie. A second operation, which severed some nerves in her neck, left her hobbling and dragging her left leg. As the cancer worsened, many operations were performed to try and alleviate her suffering. Every new regimen of antibiotics, medications and treatments intended to drive out the impending death, revealed another complication, another mass of cancer, another loss of function. The doctors continued to probe and prod and confer without finding a solution.

Frankie watched, with terrible confusion, his loving and caring mother shrivel. She never complained or was bitter during the entire time. "She was in a cage slowly being eaten alive by an invisible rat. Here was this healthy, lovely person, who never complained, slowly turning into a hobbling, horrible mess. It took everything. It is a shame what the poor undeserving woman suffered for the last seven years of her life."

Kathy remembers the wailing ambulances: "They were always there. She was always ill. She had so many operations. Mom would be home for a while. Something happened, and then the ambulance came, usually at night. I can still hear those sirens."

Meanwhile, Frank Sr.'s problems with heart disease and blood pressure escalated. Between his temper, poor diet, weight problem, drinking, stress and his "raging," he was a latent volcano. Many of his problems started when he moved from labor work to indoor work. When Frank Sr. first bought the tire store, he did much of the labor-intensive work himself. He quickly realized there wasn't any money in fixing tires. Selling tires was a more lucrative route. He hired people to do the grunt work and moved to full-time office work. He sold 1,000 tires to Canada Steamship Lines and similar companies with fleets of vehicles. The shift from physically intensive work to routine, inactive office work greatly contributed to his demise. With the move came too much stress, too much drinking, too much partying and too little exercise.

Frank Sr. was continually tormented by the paradox of his personality. One side showed a devoted family man. The other, a free spirit who liked his freedom and independence. He enjoyed trips to the family cottage where he'd find relief from the stress of a growing business. His yearly 30-day trip to Florida was a private affair, except for the week his wife Elsie joined him. On yet another side, he was building the Canadian dream. He bought a new car every two years, wore the finest clothing, had a nice home in affluent Mount Royal, and his family enjoyed every luxury. Perhaps Frank Sr. would have avoided a slaying by the killer of dreams – riches – if he had pursued his first love. "Dad should have gone into the candy business," says Frankie. "There was more skill involved. Perhaps he regretted not buying that candy business. He went into the tire business to make money."

Like a twister, Frank Sr.'s rage rose suddenly, unexpectedly, unknowingly, from nothing into explosive violence. Daily, the fury increased. It erupted, leaving everyone in ruins. "He ranted and raved. He'd have an uncontrollable fit. We lived with a nightmare. He always blew up, blaming everyone and everything for his troubles."

After his initial heart surgery, Frank Sr. went to seminars and gatherings with the heart specialists at the Montreal Jewish Hospital. He was a guinea pig, a patient who had survived the newest surgical techniques. In the '50s, doctors were trying new techniques for heart surgery. They opened a patient from the back and took out the fat tissue from the ribs. Although doing their best, there was nothing they could do to cure his heart disease. This was extremely frustrating for a man challenged by solving his own problems.

Constantly tired and irritable, Frank Sr. rested in the afternoon. "I was playing ball with my friends in the lane behind the house. We woke him up and he shouted something like 'Can't you kids go and play some place else.' " Frankie's friends' disappointment pricked like childhood inoculations.

Despite good intentions, the family's Sunday afternoon drive turned into a horrible affair. Frank Sr. heaped verbal abuse on his wife and his kids. He exploded over something trivial. An argument followed, and the family headed home, shaken, bruised and battered.

At other times, watching TV or building something, Frankie dreaded the sound of the door opening softly upstairs, two or three hours past his father's usual arrival. He feared the stumble on the stairs, the loud banging of cabinet doors, the slam of the refrigerator door. Many nights his stressed, angry, tired father picked a fight over cold dinner, disrespect, washer fluid for the car, no garbage bags, no rye bread, the wrong kind of mustard or some other insignificant thing. His tongue thick with drink, Frank Sr. fumed about stupid, petty things. He piled abuse on Kathy and Elsie. With Kathy hurt and weeping in tears, he'd finally stop. Then the family went to bed. "Why does he do that?" Frankie asked his mother.

"Oh, don't worry about it. It's just the way he is," she replied. Fulfilling "be responsible, take-charge" expectations, Frankie reasoned: "He's my father. That's the way he is. What am I going to do, run away? I'll just have to learn to live with it." To him, having two dying parents and taking such adult responsibility as a teenager, was normal. "It wasn't abnormal to me. It was normal. I didn't know anything different. I thought, 'Of course my parents are dying. Aren't everybody's?' "

Despite her grave condition and her constant pain, Elsie remained a strong, level-headed woman and the anchor of the family. Every year, for the last seven years of her life, she had a major operation. She was frequently in and out of the hospital. Feeling a responsibility to his mother, Frankie sometimes gave up his own activities. One time, after a music gig at a local college, a friend suggested it might be fun to spend time at his family's cottage. Initially, Frankie was thrilled at the idea of spending a weekend with Jill, his attractive girlfriend at the time. Remembering his dying mother at home, he declined the invitation. Frankie realized he had a tendency to live life, very intensely, very emotionally and with a heightened sense of awareness.

While Frankie's home life was a disaster, his marks slipping, occasionally lapsing into spells of depression, he found solace in his music and high school activities. Girls also helped! "It was a side of me that had been latent for so long. My goals and ambitions were going to come out. Before, I aspired to my parent's aims. Now I yearned for my own."

At the same time, music, changing values and a generational cleavage were transforming society. A great divide of experience could never be totally erased. The causes that had framed people's lives for so long, the Depression, the war and reconstruction, were fading. The breadwinners worked hard and long to afford the picture window, car, barbecue, Lionel trains. While Depression era parents were grateful for affluence, they were still haunted by poverty and scarcity memories. Many preached the "when I was your age" tales of woe. The young were tired of being reminded how bad things had been. There were expected to feel "good and grateful" to live in a prosperous country. Teenagers were not so much indifferent. Rather, they were "confused" over their parent's rigid, conservative values and their own growing need for independence.

Before the mid-1950s, children and adults shared many of the same sources of music. There was no youth or teenage culture. Now, popular music, the movies and other mass media spoke directly to the young, challenging the affluent society's claims that its social arrangements were nourishment for the human spirit. Rock 'n' roll, which started in the '50s and exploded in the '60s, was a teenager's cry of "Deliver Me From the Days of Old." Rock was rough, real, raw, compared with the music it replaced. Parents found it difficult to understand why young people could listen to salacious rock 'n' roll instead of nice, clean-cut singers. "Rock was itself a moment of abundance, energy in profusion. It was an invitation to dance, and at some fantasy level – just as the bluenoses protested – it was an invitation to make love. Even if the lyrics said so subliminally, the beat said it directly: express yourself, move yourself around, get going. Rock announced: being young means being able to feel rock. Whatever it is you're in, kid, you're not in it alone; you and your crowd are where it's at, spirited or truculent or misunderstood, and anyone who doesn't get it, is, well, square," writes Todd Gitlin in the book *The Sixties, Years of Hope, Days of Rage.*

The family no longer huddled around the living room radio console. With the advent of plastic cases and transistors, portable and cheap radios were the rage among teenagers. Even more than the saxophone or the guitar, the radio escalated the rock culture. Radio stations switched to a low-cost, audience-segmented format. Rock, magnified by jukeboxes, was ideal. Thanks to the radio, Carl Perkins, Jerry Lee Lewis, Buddy Holly and southern white boys coexisted alongside Chuck Berry, Little Richard and Fats Domino. In 1955 the airwaves rocked with Fats Domino's 'Ain't That a Shame,' Bill Haley and His Comets' 'Rock Around the Clock,' Chuck

Berry's 'Maybelline' and Little Richard's 'Tutti Frutti.' The rock 'n' roll market exploded. Formerly adult music, the blues was now directed at teenage problems: desire, jealousy, loneliness, misunderstanding by adults.

Rock was the music of choice on records, radio, at concerts and school dances. Rock movies harnessed the image of shakin', rattlin' and rollin' to teenagers' generational surge. Parents couldn't understand the *sha da da da, ba do, bay-beh, do-wop, do-wop*, or the grunting, stylizing, shrieking and whining. Leading the pack was Elvis Presley, riding a gold Cadillac, dressed in gold suits and gyrating his hips so sensuously that when he appeared on television the cameras never showed him below the waist. Parents were enraged: young people were ecstatic as he belted out 'Heartbreak Hotel,' 'Hound Dog' and 'Jail House Rock.'

Frankie's first rock 'n' roll band started when singer-guitar player Joe Padulo, the guy from Park Ex., phoned him and asked if he'd like to join a couple of guys at a high school sock hop. The group performed their first gig at the Mount Royal Recreation Centre. "I had a blast. It wasn't work. I discovered that I could have fun with music," notes Frankie. Throughout high school the Josie Padulo Band played at local colleges, schools and social events. Frankie imitated the rising stars of the era including Jerry Lee Lewis and Bill Haley. He was especially captivated by Ray Charles, the inimitable soul crooner.

"Although I enjoyed Bill Haley as much as anyone else, it wasn't long before my Father bought the *William Tell* overture, and the classics became my music. Many of my peers in Mount Royal also turned to sophisticated music. I wonder if this had more to do with IQ or the stimulating environment we grew up in." When the band wasn't performing they listened to classical music at Frankie's house. At high school graduation, Frankie had a large collection including Bach, Beethoven, Mozart, Rossini, Tchaikovsky, Chopin and Rachmaninoff.

For his 17th birthday, Elsie bought her son an MGA, a sporty English sportscar, an eye-catcher and girl catcher. "It was hot. If you were young and had a few bucks, it was a license to do whatever you wanted," recalls Frankie. On Saturday afternoon, armed with a blanket, bottle of wine and sandwiches, he took his sweetheart to the local haunt. Mount Royal Park, a city park at the summit of Mont Real, was "the" place for necking or a backseat interlude. The park is a popular all-season recreation area. In the summer Frankie strolled though its 500 acres along winding trails and walked to the summit. In the winter he cross-country skied the trails and skated on Beaver Lake, an artificially made pond.

While Frankie blundered through male-female relations, he also stumbled to the dance of grief and weeping. As his father's medical condition declined, he flew into rages several times a day, Frankie's mother on the receiving end of the abuse. One of Frank Sr.'s favorite expressions was, 'If I'm here next year, we'll get a boat (or go on a trip).' Confused and fearful, his son asked himself, "What does he mean if he's here next year?"

While Kathy was away at band practice and Elsie at the women's club, Frankie frequently found his father in the bathroom, rolling on the floor in agony and vomiting in the toilet. He watched his once-handsome features blur by years of stress, booze and anguish. Frankie gave him nitroglycerin pills. "I think he knew something was wrong, that he had two or three years to live. He didn't tell anyone. He said it was his heart. But I knew something else was wrong, seeing him in such agony." Unknown to the family, Frank Sr. developed leukemia.

On Friday, March 7, 1959, Frankie visited his father in Montreal's Royal Victoria Hospital. The 56-year-old face was pale and creased. Two days later, Frank Sr. phoned home to check on the family. In his usual manner he asked, "How's school? How are things? Take care of your mother." Even after years of seeing death as a constant companion, Frankie was inconsolable when his father died at 6:00 a.m., Monday, March 10, 1959; "I knew this man was on his death bed. But it still hit me hard. I was totally destroyed." Frankie's mother was equally disconsolate and overcome with emotion. Her tears were complex: sadness over losing her husband and partner, relief that his suffering had ended, comfort in knowing that the abuse was over. Ironically, marriage to Frank Sr. had given her shape and had held her. With his passing, she was suddenly set free, like Jell-O taken from its mold too soon.

Fooled by his aura of responsibility, everyone thought that Frankie could handle his father's death. "I was always the success. No one thought it would affect me. Little Frankie was an old man who could handle anything. It was expected. I was the president of every club. I was supposed to just waltz though it. But I was devastated. I carried the responsibility well. I didn't let anybody know I was suffering. It wasn't until many years later that I had to wrestle with this burden. Frank had died. Frankie would have to become Frank overnight. He inherited both the very best and the very worst of the man he loved in anguish. Quiet storms were building on a distant horizon, dark clouds would become the forewarning of disaster," recalls Frank.

He laced his running shoes, pulled on his sweatshirt and pounded the asphalt until his throat seared with the struggle of breathing. Sweat, disguising his pain and grief, trickled and taunted his legs, chest, arms and back. At dawn, the streets of Mount Royal were quiet, except for the thud of his shoes on the pavement in perfect rhythm that made him feel that living through another day was bearable. Running helped to ease the sting of his father's death and slightly dim the haunting picture of his bedridden mother slowly turning into a brittle-boned shadow. He'd run four, sometimes five miles, the sun coming up over the cross at the top of Mont Real, past familiar streets with landmarks to guide him: the orange tabby, perched so unflappable in the neighbor's window; St. Peter's Anglican Church on the corner; the quarter-mile track that sat, cinder-grey and sunburnt between Carlyle School and Mount Royal High; on neighbor's lawns, plastic gnomes, deer, and geese stationed between a grove of yellow plastic sunflowers with whirligig petals. His face was flushed and healthy, covered with a glaze of wetness. His daily running culminated in a moment of glory when he placed tenth in a six-mile run at the high school track and field meet.

With high school nearing completion, an obligatory photo and message was needed for the yearbook. Frank's listing in the 1959 *Torch* read:

MILLS, FRANK WILLIAM (MILLS)

"Exams to me are a lot of bunkum. Bunkum or not,
I better not flunkum."
Origin: Montreal, Quebec, June 27, 1942
Favorite Expression: "Oh, so cool!"
Prototype: "In the mood" – with the Bulawayo Sweet Rhythms Band.
Unrecorded History: Once played a drum solo in a geometry period.
Ambition: To enter the tire business.
Probable destination: See you at the next blowout.
Activities: Senior Band 1956-'59; Glee Club 1957-'59; Student Council Executive 1957-'59; Ski Club 1956-'59; Executive 1957-'59; Camera Club Executive 1957-'58.

In May 1959, three months after his father's death, Frank gave the valedictory address: "Mr. Chairman, distinguished guests, Mr. Drysdale, members of the staff, ladies and gentlemen, and fellow graduates:

During the past four years, we, the members of the graduating class of 1959 of Mount Royal High School, have lived as a family. We have learned to bear with one another and to respect the rights of the individual within the family unit. We have learned to respect authority and to accept with grace the discipline which must exist within any society. But more than this, we have learned to accept and bear the responsibilities entrusted to us, for surely, this is the yardstick of maturity and citizenship.

The head of our family was Mr. Drysdale who encouraged us to live up to the motto of our school and to extract the ultimate benefit from it. When we went astray, we found Miss Dombroski and Mr. Anderson, always eager to lend a little more encouragement. As well, on our family tree were the fine teachers who were responsible for guiding us in so many ways and instilling in us a greater love of learning. We must also thank those who so efficiently ran our home during our stay here and kept us in healthy and fresh surroundings.

Four years ago, we arrived, young and timid children, lost in the empty corridors, looking for some form of security to which we could cling. School tradition supplied that security. I suppose our school crest best exemplifies the object of our search, for Mount Royal High's shield is one of hope for physical and moral courage. Within our shield is a crown, a crown of loyalty to our school. A broad band supports three glowing torches; one represents knowledge, the purpose of formal education. The second represents wisdom, the goal of all sincere seekers. The third represents kindness, certainly the atmosphere of Mount Royal during our time here. Under the crest is the motto of our school: TUM SIT TOLLERE IN ALTUM – BE YOURS TO HOLD IT HIGH. For four years, we have carried this torch and to us it was admiration, for it was lighted by those who have gone before, many of whom who hoped that it might be kept burning. I like to think that the accent is on the word "yours," stressing the responsibility of the individual. This, however, is not a torch we can lay aside now that we are about to leave the school; rather, it is one that we will carry with us as a light on our paths and a beacon for those who follow.

As we became acquainted with our school, its staff and fellow students four long years ago, we participated in many activities that Mount Royal High School offered. We traveled in groups of 50 and 100 to Potsdam,

Ottawa, Burlington and points as far away as Rhode Island. On these excursions our neighbors south of the border welcomed our arrival and our departure. The music department recently spent a weekend in Burlington (I personally don't recall hearing too much band music); however, the trip was one of utmost enjoyment. Undoubtedly, we shall miss taking part in the plays and operettas that we performed on so enthusiastically (not to mention the parties afterwards). We shall miss seeing the beautiful costumes and scenery that graced our stage frequently during the past, and the bright shining faces....that arrived on Friday morning after Thursday night's performance.

In future, we shall look back on our high school pranks as things that made life so enjoyable – for the students of course, for we never did anything original like our parents. Some slightly older friends of mine told me that they used to set the clocks forward in class to be dismissed five minutes early. We were let out five minutes early all right, but the next day we received forty minutes' detention for arriving five minutes late. Either teachers today are smarter than they used to be or the students are....no, that couldn't be right... "the child is father of the man."

These are the things that we shall tell our children as we have been told by our parents. When we tell of our school, we can definitely be proud of it. Sincerely, we have been fortunate to come into contact with such a pleasant and understanding staff.

Our past at Mount Royal High School has been a fruitful one and our future has been well prepared for us. We shall miss the kind staff of our school who acted as secondary parents. We shall also miss each other. Our departure is, indeed, a sad one but Mount Royal High School will never be forgotten. Throughout our lives we shall remember the friendly school at the foot of Mount Royal and daily we shall use the benefits we have derived from it. With our strong foundation, we shall be watched by parents and teachers alike who hope today that we shall prove worthy of their efforts. Throughout adulthood we shall be alone, unguided by our teachers and left to make decisions on our own. There will be a day when our paths shall cross again. Together we will talk of our youthful days at Mount Royal. Thus, to Mount Royal we shall never bid farewell. Forever we shall use the benefits of our four years, and forever we shall carry Mount Royal High School's brilliant torch. TUM SIT TOLLERE IN ALTUM – BE YOURS TO HOLD IT HIGH."

Frank's View

How to Get Kids to Practice

"You have to practice before you can watch television."

"Hurry up. How come you're always so slow to get to your music lesson."

"No dessert until you've got your lessons done."

" No, you can't go to Sally's sleep-over until you've practiced."

"If you don't practice you can't go to the zoo."

The sounds of coaxing and pleading and bartering may not be music to a child's ear. In fact, there is a kinder, gentler and more effective way to get kids to practice. Music rounds out personality and character. It helps build life skills. It helps reinforce the benefits of persistence over time. A child will learn that he can accomplish much – playing in the school band, at a concert, for a recital, a contest – by practicing a little bit each day. If the child is continually resistant, hates the lessons, and struggles with practicing, it's a waste of time and money. If the child likes the piano but hates to practice, he needs assistance, guidance and rewards for developing good practice habits. Each case is a different problem, requiring a different solution. Playing and practicing the piano or other instrument should be fun. Above all, encourage the child through praise, fun and support.

* *Establish a practice time* (15 minutes a day is adequate for a beginner). Praise the child before, during and after the session. If he wants to play more, encourage that. If he wants to play ball with friends, that's okay, too.
* *When a child shows interest, start lessons.* While a parent or teacher can encourage that interest, the motive must be something that comes from within the child. Formal lessons usually begin at around eight years old. If a child shows special interest (playing the piano himself, asking how to play an instrument) five isn't too young.
* *Choose a teacher wisely.* Lessons can be drudgery if the student doesn't like the teacher.
* *Avoid cramming the day before lessons.* Cramming often indicates a dislike for something. If it's a constant problem to get the

child to practice, the problem may be a lack of interest in formal lessons.

* *Encourage creativity.* Listen to the compositions. Ask questions. Ask the child to repeat the number, faster, slower, softer. Thank him for playing. You can quickly destroy creativity by criticizing, pushing or plodding.
* *Create a music-friendly home.* Encourage the child to listen to different music. Take them to concerts, shows, music performances. Encourage him to imitate the songs he hears and also to invent his own tunes. Encourage singing, creativity, experimentation and playing at home. Some children may want to learn about a favorite musician's life. Encourage a child to "conduct" to the pieces he hears.
* *Encourage the child to try a variety of instruments.* Pound a drum, play a clarinet, plunk on a keyboard. The child will enjoy the experience and likely discover the instrument he likes best.
* *Help develop personal sensitivity.* Encourage the child to trust his feelings and sensitivities to music. Ask him how the music feels. A closer connection to music can bring a more enjoyable experience.
* *Encourage music activities.* Suggest musical ventures like the school band, ensemble, choral groups, etc. Making friends with people who share music interests is especially important. Young children have a strong need to feel a part of something and to contribute to group activities.
* *Make music fun.* Take the seriousness out of recitals, exams and practicing. Ensure a child has lots of other activities to round out his childhood. Encourage him to try sports, friends and hobbies. While discipline must be applied to encourage kids, avoid ramming lessons and recitals down their throat. The child will come to hate music and buckle under the pressure. Pleasure is the key to success in anything.

For two summers after his father's death, Frank worked at his father's tire shop. The first summer, he worked on the floor, fitting the pressure gauges on a compressor, fixing flats on cars and on eight and sixteen wheelers. "There I was, under a 40-foot truck trying to get the spare tire out. It was rusted and coated with muck. I'd whack it with a sledge hammer. All the dirt and crud crashed on me. It was awful. Here was a piano player slugging tires. It just didn't fit." Frank Sr. would have taken special enjoyment in seeing his son get his hands soiled when removing grimy, muddied tires from vehicles. "Dad had always hoped that my brother would take over the business. While music meant everything to him, I don't think he was thinking of it as a career," says Kathy.

The second summer, Frank worked in the office answering phones, taking orders, handling cash and dealing with customers. His music interests were seen as hobbies. Although Frank Sr. had been proud of his son, encouraging his musical interests, he had frequently told him: "You won't make any money at music, musicians are always in the poor house." After finishing his shift at the tire shop, Frank Jr. strolled over to Biere Depinette de chez nous, at the corner of Notre Dame Street and Montagne, where he dished out eighty-five cents for two hot dogs and a spruce beer.

Shortly after Frank Sr.'s death, Kathy met and married Terry Stone. The newlyweds moved away to leave Frank Jr. and the Jamaican maid to care for Elsie. The Pauly family, who lived down the street from the Mills home, invited Frank to join the family on their two-week Christmas/New Year vacation to Lac Tremblant, a wilderness area in the Laurentians, about three hours north of Montreal. Mont Tremblant, the highest of the Laurentian peaks (3,150 ft/960 metres) is the main feature of Quebec's most popular recreational area. Algonquin Indians called their mountain Manitonga Soutana (Devil's Mountain or Trembling Mountain) because it roared and rumbled whenever the tranquillity of its forested slopes were disturbed. Frank fell in love with this wilderness area that would serve him well in his later years. With $10,000, his inheritance from the sale of the tire shop, he bought two lots on the shores of Lac Tremblant for $4,500 each. Fairy Falls, the 15-acre lot with its trickling stream, glens and clusters of wild mint growing in the field, resembled Ireland. The other lot comprised 100 acres of Quebec bush land.

In December 1960, the dining room of the Mills home was turned into a hospital room. In the last year of her life, Elsie Mills lived in the dining room, just off the living room. With the aid of an overhead bar, she'd lift herself so Frank could change her dressings. Kathy visited several times each week. Elsie's sisters, Kitty and Gladys, provided much needed assistance. From her deathbed, frail Elsie planned meals, gave directions to the maid and parented Frank. "I think we should talk about sex," said the 53-year-old.

"It's okay, Mom. I've read a lot about that. And I've talked to some people. You don't have to worry," Frank told her. On the deathwatch he gave her morphine injections every four hours. His mother's grotesque features left their imprint upon him: her red-rimmed eyes, stood so eerily in the darkness, her dry flaky skin, patchy like a moth-eaten sweater. The changing light on the folds of her sheets was the only sign of movement. Frank listened to his mother's breath, her features distorted with the effort of straining for yet another gasp of life. When her dreadful breathing stopped, he was relieved, confused, shocked at the hideous silence which ensued. There had been little time to heal in the weeks between his father's death and his mother's decline. Frank's feelings were a hopeless jumble, when on December 23, 1960, his mother died. The funeral home was called and two men came, with black suits, soft voices and a collapsible gurney to take away her body. Elsie's bed in the dining room stood empty by the window. As Frank opened the curtains, the sun fell upon the white sheets that had been changed the day before. His griefs were too numerous, too confused, too complex.

He built his life around her. Now what happens when she disappears? Where does he go? Into pieces, into atoms, into infinity. He cried, screamed, slept, walked. He wasn't really there. He was someplace else trying to make sense of it all. When he squinted his eyes he thought he saw her in the shadows beyond the trees, in the front yard, in the kitchen baking butterscotch oatmeal cookies. The unfinished business of that loss would later haunt him. There was no story he could tell himself that made sense of how or why death had stolen his father, and now his mother. To young Frank his mother was kind, optimistic, supportive with a lovely, gentle temperament. She had been the anchor, the rock of the family who kept affairs together despite horrific circumstances. Now, he was robbed, betrayed, abandoned. His sensitive nature was angry and confused, smarting at the change of fortune that was shaping the world around him.

For Frank, music offered hope, release, comfort – a voice for his anguished soul. The record player in the living room that played music at the wrong speed was nearly worn out from his listening, hour after hour, to Sergei Rachmaninoff's music. He listened to the music and played it on the piano, his head tilted as if hearing some inner imprint of that music. In the familiar sequences of notes Frank heard his own pain and rage. Death's hidden secrets were the inspiration for some of Rachmaninoff's finest music. The Russian composer's 83 works express sensitive emotions ranging from fatalistic resignation, outbursts of wild despair, exquisite sensitivity to the beauties of nature and romantic longings. When asked to state what music was, Rachmaninoff said: "What is music? How can one define it? Music is a calm moonlit night, a rustling of summer foliage. Music is the distant peal of bells at eventide. Music is born only of the heart and it appeals to the heart. It is love. The sister of music is poetry and the mother – sorrow!"

Frank was especially fond of Rachmaninoff's piece 'Concerto No. 2 in C Minor, (Op. 18).' Its almost unbroken lyricism and unprecedented elements of sadness, nostalgia and sincerity account for its phenomenal popularity. The song has been plagiarized by songwriters around the world. It has been suggested that many people still attribute to Rachmaninoff the songs 'Full Moon and Empty Arms,' 'Ever and Forever,' 'If This is Good-bye' and 'This is my Kind of Love.' Eric Carmen was sued because his song 'All by Myself' was so close to Rachmaninoff's version.

Rachmaninoff wrote the piece after a bout of depression and lack of confidence. Unable to make a start on the concerto, he fell into a state of melancholy and despair. His Aunt Varvara, who had been helped by hypnosis, recommended the treatment to her nephew. Dr. Nikolai Dahl induced Rachmaninoff into a state of hypnotic sleep. He told him he would soon recover his lost confidence, that he would begin to write a new concerto and that it would prove to be an excellent piece. It would be far better than anything he had previously composed. The treatment was successful and Rachmaninoff dedicated the concerto to Dr. Dahl.

Like Rachmaninoff, Frank found music and songwriting comforting in a time of great despair: "It was just starting to happen. I was looking for an outlet, a relief. I had written a lot of depressing poetry. Now, this was moving into songs, both lyrics and instrumental pieces." At the time, however, songwriting was largely a hobby for a troubled young man trying to cope with the loss of both parents.

Recognizing the young man's plight, caring neighbors offered support. The Close family – Mr. Close, Marjorie Close and their three sons John, Nick and Toni and daughter Jennie – were important to him during the rough years surrounding his parents' illness and eventual death. Frank skied, hiked and traveled with the family and had a teenage romance with Jennie.

Dr. Fred Woolhouse, a native of Saskatchewan and plastic surgeon who lived around the corner, frequently invited him over for Sunday dinner, and he played the piano in return. Dr. Woolhouse, a member of the Green Lake Fish and Game Club on Green Lake near Annunciation, Quebec, hired the young man as a gilly (Scottish name for fishing guide and gopher). For two summers, Frank accompanied a group of doctors on their fishing adventures. He cooked, cleaned, replenished the boats, emptied the torpedoes (the container that stored live fish) and did grunt work. On calm waters, Frank paddled his canoe to the loon's lonely cry, the dazzling sun setting in the horizon and maples leafing in the distance. He'd catch 10-20 trout hidden in the evening shadows.

After Elsie's death, Kathy and Terry and their first son, Ted, came to live with Frank in the family home that had been left to both children. When Dr. Woolhouse heard that Frank wanted to be a doctor, he invited him into his office. Frank watched, with anticipation and excitement the display of rebuilds. To the eager onlooker, Dr. Woolhouse was a craftsman, an architect of a different sort. He didn't work with oils, woods, floorplans, charcoal, on a drafting table or behind a sewing machine. Rather, Dr. Woolhouse rebuilt and aligned faces that lost firm contours, he reconstructed faces damaged by accident, disease or heredity. He gave people hope. However, for Frank to get into McGill University he had to raise his 72 percent average. In the fall of 1961, after repeating grade eleven and raising his average to 82 percent, he was accepted into the Bachelor of Science program at McGill University in Montreal. The hands that loved to tinker, fix things and put things back together, might change the world. Frank was off to find himself. Hopefully, he might alleviate some of the suffering his parents had endured. "It was cadavers, here we come."

3

SUCCESS BY ACCIDENT

McGill University rests in the heart of Montreal, its gates open onto the city's financial, commercial and retail arteries – Sherbrooke Street, McGill College Avenue and Ste. Catherine Street. Old houses, with their romantic towers, high front steps, shuttered windows, gables and elaborate gingerbread trim, are sandwiched between soaring skyscrapers and tucked away in the leafy corners of the campus. At McGill, lush, 20-year-old Virginia Creepers cascade from the rooftops of libraries, fraternity houses, concert halls, auditoriums and student residences. The rich scent of blooming lilac hedges suffuse the air. It is a place of learning, limestone and reputation, like an ancient Arthurian Kingdom with its historic buildings and sacred lecture halls, its aura of grand and noble undertakings.

Within a ten-minute walk of the campus are theatres, cinemas, art galleries, museums and Metro – Montreal's subway with underground corridors linking office towers and shopping centres throughout the downtown core. A large collection of 18th and 19th century buildings on cobblestone streets lead to Parisian-style cafes, gourmet-food shops, galleries, clothing boutiques, restaurants and bakeries. Montreal possesses something of an Old World flavor while remaining resolutely part of the New World. The city is the cradle of Quebec's nationalism and vigorously cosmopolitan citizenry. Half of Quebec's residents live within viewing distance of either the St. Lawrence River or Mont Real. The city is a patchwork of distinct quarters – ethnic neighborhoods such as the Jewish quarter, Chinatown, a Portuguese area, English-speaking Westmount and French-speaking Outremont – that engender a village atmosphere within the boundaries of a great metropolis. With its curious dialect (17th century French with injections of 20th century English), Montreal maintains its own, distinctive Frenchness, enriched by an influx of immigrants from all over the world. This city is the home of language wars, faded grandeur and a fast-talking way of life. With such a diverse cultural background, it's not surprising that Montreal is frequently called the city with two faces. It presents a formal image to the rest of the world. The other face is the informal manner its inhabitants adopt with each other.

The faces in Dr. Woolhouse's office that had once inspired Frank to pursue medicine, faded quickly. He spent more time sleeping and playing in the band than learning about medicine with the cadavers. When a serious depression lingered, his marks dropped, he missed many classes, and goofed off. A torrid love affair added to the growing calamity and confusion. Kathy remembers seeing a disgruntled brother: "He was doing his thing, college, girlfriend. He was always involved with music. But we knew he really didn't like his studies. It was hard for him."

Much to his surprise, Frank failed an English course during his first year. He thought he should have done well in the subject considering Dr. Buchanan's influence in high school. During his first summer at McGill he worked for the Iron Ore Company of Canada in Northern Labrador. With little to do in a mining town, Frank decided he'd re-do the failed course over the summer. "I loved it. I studied books and poetry, all the stuff we had brushed over in class a few months before. I got into it for my own interest, not to pass an exam," notes Frank. He flew to Montreal on the company plane and wrote the exam. Back at work a day later, he'd forgotten about the course and carried on with his summer job. At McGill for second year, he saw his passing grade on the bulletin board. When his English teacher walked by, Frank asked for more explanation. "The instructor told me that on a supplemental exam of four questions with 25 marks each, they went through the exam until you got a pass. If they went through all four questions and still didn't get 50 percent, you failed. He said, 'I read your answers to the first two questions, and you passed.' While I had studied hard for that English exam and proved to myself that I could do it, there was an attitude problem. One more paradox! I knew I could do it, so why bother? I wasn't going to do something that wasn't a challenge. It was the child coming out in me."

On the side, Frank kept writing songs. He wrote the instrumental piece 'Peter Piper Goes to Church' (later changed to 'Peter Piper') for his nephew, Ted. His cheerful, little godson frequently sat on his uncle's lap while he played. Frank's piece '401 West' paid homage to the many hours he spent on Highway 401 commuting between Montreal and Toronto. Kathy and Terry had two more children and Frank frequently baby-sat. He found the house too crowded. Seeking peace and quiet, he moved into the fraternity Delta Upsilon (Greek DU), an old house with wrought iron stairs in the back, gabled roofs and stone steps on McTavish Street on the McGill campus.

Frank's social, gregarious side developed while his academic side suffered. He couldn't see any sense in studying Latin, Calculus and Botany. He wanted to use his hands, his tinkering skills. By second year, his 40 percent grade reflected his growing frustration and disillusionment. The academic side of medicine destroyed his lofty ambitions of becoming a doctor. In his mind, doctors were "glorified chemists." Dean Stansbury, head of the science faculty, called Frank into his office and gave him the boot. "I knew these hands were talented. If there had been an apprentice route to becoming a doctor, rather than the academic route, I would have been a great surgeon today. Botany? Who needs that? Let me work with my hands," Frank muses. "I probably could have given more to the world as a surgeon than I have through music."

Uncertain about his future, Frank decided to join the Canadian Navy. The recruiting office, on the same street as the Fraternity, was a few doors up from the Faculty of Music. As Frank was passing by the faculty, Bill Walker, his friend in the high school band, flung open the doors. "Hey, Rach. I haven't seen you in a while. What's happening?" asked Bill (He always called his friend 'Rach' after Frank's most beloved composer, Rachmaninoff). Frank explained that he'd just been thrown out of medical school and was on his way to join the navy.

"Rach, you can't do that. Come on in," and Bill dragged Frank into the building. He took him on a tour of the Music Faculty and suggested his friend should take the entrance requirements, a written exam and performance on two instruments. Frank aced the written exam with 96 percent. He earned credit for his first instrument with a rousing rendition on the trombone. Caught off guard for his second instrument, he told admissions officer Istvan Anhalt he'd been tinkering with Rachmaninoff's 'Second Piano Concerto No. 2.' With a thick Hungarian accent that frequently needed repeating what he spoke, Anhalt laughed after he heard the young man's interpretation. "Is there something wrong?" asked Frank.

"Oh no, loovely, loovely. You're gott good err. Gott play. But vie ewe play in C *sharrrp mineer*?" asked Anhalt.

"That's the way I've always heard it," shrugged Frank.

"You see sheet musak?"

"No. I've only played along with the record player."

"Wrote in key of C *mineer*," chuckled Anhalt.

Frank had never seen the music score. If he had, he would have played the piece in its intended key, C *minor*. In fact, the turntable, moving too fast, had bumped the concerto into C *sharp* minor. Without knowing it, Frank had become proficient in playing in the dreaded key, the one with seven sharps and only two white notes. "I vant you in mine musak class," insisted Anhalt. Fortunately, Anhalt convinced Dean Helmut Blume, head of the music faculty, that the ex-wanna-be doctor should be allowed back into McGill. Frank likely holds the honor of being the only student kicked out of McGill and reinstated in less than one hour.

"In the early '60s, we had forty students and were housed in a variety of somewhat rundown, old houses on the edge of the campus. Today, with 700 students, the Faculty is the largest in Canada and, by many measures, the best," says Richard Lawton, dean, faculty of music, McGill University. Frank and Hugh Hartwell, the only two students in Anhalt's composition class that year, occasionally lunched together and reveled in the works of modern electronic composers. In frat garb, straight Frank wore a blue collared shirt with fraternity tie, brown jacket, jeans and Bassweejuns loafers. "Most of the kids in the Music Faculty dressed funny and wore horned-rimmed glasses. You could tell which faculty students were in by the way they dressed. When I told people I was in music, they gave me this funny look. Music students were supposed to look weird," remembers Frank.

The music student appeared to be fine. He carried the familiar torch of responsibility and ended up running the fraternity house for about a year. Psychologically speaking, however, he was a mess. At times, in utter despair, it was difficult to get out of bed. Sometimes he slept for two or three days. When he got up, he struggled with the day's attire. Shirt? Sweater? Jacket? Tie? Pants? Still listening to Rachmaninoff's music, Frank realized he was sinking further. Fortunately, a psychiatrist who had moved into the fraternity gave counseling in exchange for residents' views on fraternity life. He hypnotized Frank a few times and helped to alleviate some of his distress.

The wounds, however, still festered. While Frank should have been concentrating on his education, music played an important, but detrimental role in his college life. He co-wrote the scores for the 1964 and 1965 *Red and White Review*, a yearly theatre satire produced and performed by the students of McGill. Fraternity life was a juggle of gigs, girls and guzzling. "The McGill College Band – me, a drummer and two guitar players – played the three to six p.m. TGIF (Thank God it's Friday) gig. After a few beers it was another gig that lasted until three in the morning. I'd play in the McGill Marching Band on Saturday afternoon. We'd do another gig on Saturday night." The $200-$300 he earned for each gig, plus a small inheritance, carried him through college.

The Beatles changed the face of rock 'n' roll during the '60s. Songs such as 'She Loves You,' 'I Want to Hold Your Hand,' 'Can't Buy me Love,' and 'A Hard Day's Night,' which drew from Elvis's rock 'n' roll, country music and the blues, elevated the primitive power of rock from a barbaric tom-tom beat to a sophisticated art form. The Rolling Stones followed with 'I Can't Get no Satisfaction,' 'No Expectations,' 'Sympathy for the Devil' and 'Stray Cat Blues.' Inebriated Frank impersonated these greats of the day. He rendered a wicked Ray Charles imitation, complete with blackened face. "I burnt a cork and smeared it everywhere. I was as black as the ace of spades." Ray Charles remains one of Frank's favorite musicians because of his soulful, meaningful way of imparting the human experience. Charles, the high priest of soul, has a voice like an old set of tubes. The *ooh, heerh, yoo, eeaiee, yawya, haay, ahhh* of his gritty, gravelly, scratchy voice exudes pain, happiness, joy and soul. "I was born with music inside me...Music was one of my parts – like my blood. It was a necessity for me – like food or water. And from the moment I learned that there were piano keys to be mashed, I started mashing 'em, trying to make sounds out of feelings," writes Charles in his autobiography, *Brother Ray*.

Frank and the band roared with a fiendish zeal, like a fistful of raw red meat jammed into the face. In the wee hours of the morning, when every soul should have been squeezed dry, the band was up on that tiny, smoke-shrouded stage, lashing out an unearthly fury. They plugged in, turned on and blasted out a blizzard of licks so fast and furious that it left everyone astonished. Thinking back, Frank is surprised that the roof didn't cave in: "I'd mimic Ray Charles' 'What I Say' and we'd go on for about 45 minutes, non-stop. Then we'd do the Rolling Stones and the Beatles. It was party time. The floor bounced." Michael Richards, fraternity brother and budding young attorney, prophesied that one day Frank would make a lot of money and he would have to move him to a tax haven. Frank is still in contact with other fraternity brothers: Jack Giacomelli (dentist in Montreal); George Elliott (lawyer in Toronto); Duncan Moran (dentist in Bermuda); John Walker (businessman in London, Ontario).

College, music and the fraternity sustained Frank. He could almost forget his pain. Yet, he rarely divulged his own secrets. "Even though I was psychologically destroyed, there was this excitement, music, friends and the fraternity. College was a womb. The fraternity was one of the main reasons I survived without needing serious psychiatric help. It was a rich spawning ground. I was searching for answers. Who was Frank? A musician? A businessman?" reflects Frank.

During the summers of his final years at McGill, Frank worked as a chef at the Hospitality Inn in Haliburton, Ontario, in cottage country about two hours north of Toronto. The manager of the hotel, George Elliot, a Delta Upsilon fraternity brother, rounded up several friends to run the lodge. Frank volunteered to feed the 100-150 guests. Peter Batson, a friend to Frank and George, visited the crew several times during the summer. "There was Frank, in his typical manner putting a sense of humor into everything he does," recalls Peter Batson. A running competition developed between a group of American tourists (the Aquasnowskiers) from Rochester, New York and the Canadians running the lodge. The harmless fun started with water fights, progressed to skiing and then to the King of the Day award. "In retaliation, Frank served them, but the food turned out looking like 'something else.' When they bit into the burgers they'd find pieces of paper stuck to their teeth," laughs Peter. Bored on Saturday nights, Frank and George ventured to nearby Minden, a small town with a grungy, gritty bar. Frank, alias "Snake," pounded on the ivories while George, alias "Rattler," railed on the drums. "Snake and the Fourskins" (the name of two-man band) got paid all the beer they could drink.

Frank remembers one McGill music professor telling the class: "If you are looking for a career where you will become rich and famous, you're in the wrong place. Most performers and composers (including the greats of Bach, Beethoven and Brahms) did not become famous or rich or even moderately successful during their lifetimes." After two years in the Music Faculty, earning a Licentiate in Music, Frank decided he'd learned enough and left to pursue a career in business.

In 1965, still considering music a hobby, Frank sold industrial chemicals at Liquid Carbonic Canadian Corporation (Union Carbide) in Montreal. He was dubbed the "singing salesman" for his performances at the company's office parties. After hours, Frank earned his pilots license. He let the license lapse after a few flights. Mr. Fix-it is proud of the welder's certificate he earned while at the company.

Although his father's urgings to pursue business still lingered, he was unhappy. "I repeatedly thought about my father during those days and remembered what he became. I saw the drudgery. I'd saw him destroy himself by doing something he didn't like. I swore to myself I wasn't going to end up like him," reflects Frank. A personality assessment prepared by Caress, Gilhooly and Kestin Inc., on Frank, revealed the mismatch:

"*Recommendation*: Mills is not recommended as a territory salesman of industrial gases with Liquid Carbonic Canadian Corporation.

Summary Reasons for Recommendation: Although Mills has an interest in selling, the probabilities are that if he would fit into sales at all, it would be in some kind of inside job selling in a store or over the counter. Mills, also, despite his excellent mechanical comprehension, does not reflect the interest pattern typical of the potentially effective industrial salesman. He just does not seem to reflect the same kind of "he-man" interests, reactions, likes, dislikes and attitudes typical of the man who fits in easily in industrial selling because he shares the interests and attitudes of the kind of people on whom he calls and to whom and through whom he must be able to sell if he is going to be effective in selling industrial gases.

Mills reflects some elements of immaturity. He is low in sense of responsibility for sticking with jobs or assignments until they are completed and low in capacity for follow through. Unlike many men who do have the basic temperament for field sales, Mills does not reflect the confidence or "cockiness of youth" that we often find in men in his age bracket who apply for outside selling jobs. He does not even appear to have much confidence in his ability to handle himself effectively in the field, to "find his way around" in his territory. Mills is unhappy. He is likely to react very emotionally to job pressures. He has marked feelings of inferiority which may not appear on the surface but of which he is very much aware. He does not think of himself as a particularly vigorous or energetic individual."

Other points in the report said: "difficulty fitting in with customers," "satisfactory ratings for human relations skills but has no feeling at all for selling," and "Mills has excellent mechanical comprehension. It certainly seems somewhat strange that here we have a man who has a primary interest in selling and no sales comprehension and who has no interest at all along production or manufacturing or engineering lines and yet who has excellent mechanical comprehension." After seeing the report, Frank's boss, Paul Dawson, suggested that the lucrative field of industrial real estate, where people and personality skills were needed, would be more suitable.

By now, his inheritance had been used. After two years with Union Carbide, Frank took Dawson's advice and sold industrial real estate for A.E. Lepage Real Estate. "I was going to work for a couple of years to save up enough money to go into music. To write. To do what I really wanted to do," recalls Frank. In March 1969, with $30,000 stashed, he informed his boss, Lorne Cook, that he was going to join a band. "Lorne looked at me and said 'You've got to be crazy. You could be vice-president.' I said, 'I didn't know that, but thanks anyway. Music is my life and that's what I'm going to do.' "

The gig he'd lined up blew apart three months later. Joe Padulo, now the owner of a model agency and several related businesses in New York, phoned Frank to ask him if he'd like to polish and groom the Sirocco Singers, a three-girl act. For three months, the group toured in New York and Newfoundland and then disbanded. "Three months after leaving A.E. Lepage I was out of work. I could almost hear Lorne laughing in the background."

Two days later Cliff Edwards of The Bells, a Canadian pop group of the era, phoned and asked Frank if he wanted to play piano with the group. Based out of Montreal, the Five Bells were appearing on the US and Canadian club circuit when publisher Bob Hahn sent them a song called 'Moody Manitoba Morning,' written by Rick Neufeld. They recorded it for Polydor Records and it came out in late 1968. It wasn't particularly successful but the band continued to record, establishing itself after they changed the name to The Bells when Anne Edwards left the band to become a mother. Both their songs 'Fly Little White Dove Fly' and 'Stay Awhile' became a top ten hit in both the US and Canada in 1971. The lineup included Cliff Edwards and his sister Jackie Ralphs, Doug Gravelle (drums), Charlie Clark,

Michael Waye and Frank on keyboards. Frank played his first show with The Bells at the Hotel Bonaventure in Montreal. On another gig, a television show taping before a live audience, the six band members and a grand piano were stuffed onto a small stage. To the arpeggio and crescendo at the end of 'Fly Little White Dove Fly,' the legs on the piano stool slipped off the stage. The crowd wailed as Frank tumbled onto the pile of curtains below. Fortunately, the crumpled fabric avoided injury and the audience thought it was part of the act.

The smell of stale beer and sweat lingered in the smoke-filled cabarets, back alley nightclubs, and grungy dives they played. In a seedy barroom, aka Mafia den, the owner was indicted for murder several days after the group's performance. At others, barely clad, high-heeled ladies solicited clients. Gruff and brazen characters were regular guests at these establishments. Irregular cash was a departure from the biweekly Union Carbide paycheck. For two or three weeks' work Frank earned considerable cash. When the gigs evaporated, he quickly learned about the feast then famine music business. However, a $1,300 royalty cheque, for three of his songs that had aired for three months, convinced him there was a gold mine in the music industry.

Despite the wretched places, Frank gained street smarts about the road, the music business and performing. Cliff Edwards suggested he secure copyright on all his compositions. Frank learned about the heady world of performing rights and reproduction rights and became a member of P.R.O. Canada (Performing Rights Organization of Canada, which was later changed to SOCAN, Society of Composers, Authors and Music Publishers of Canada). The 1998 edition of *SOCAN facts* lists the role of this performing rights society: "SOCAN is the labor-saving middleman between the copyright owner and the music user. Under the terms of the Copyright Act, SOCAN collects tariff fees from the users on behalf of its members and international copyright owners it represents in Canada. These fees are then systematically distributed as performance royalties to creators and publishers whose works have been performed, and which SOCAN has identified and credited through its own procedures. When your work is performed and identified overseas, SOCAN forwards the monies received from international societies directly to you, the copyright owner. And when an international work is performed here, SOCAN sends royalties to the copyright owner's own domestic society."

"SOCAN (formerly Broadcast Music Industry) is perhaps the major and most reliable source of income to a songwriter. SOCAN and its world affiliates monitor performances on radio and TV of all things musical. These royalties are tabulated and paid on a pay-per-play basis by a very sophisticated formula, and every member, affiliate writer or publisher is paid his share on a quarterly basis. Typical earnings of a very big hit song can pay millions of dollars worldwide over the life of the copyright to the writer-publisher," adds Frank.

Since The Bells did a lot of recording, Frank spent much time in the studio, learning the new multi-track recording system. He became friendly with the salespeople, receptionists and executives of Polydor (later named Polygram) in their Montreal office. A conversation with Guy Bertrand, Polydor's vice-president, in a restaurant washroom boosted Frank's confidence. "Guy, the group's getting ready to leave so I've got to do this quick. I'm thinking of leaving The Bells and doing an instrumental album. What do you think?" asked Frank, zipping up his fly.

"I'll release anything you do, just bring it to me," responded Guy, fastening his belt. Future prospects were quickly fading after the group's two major hits in 1971. Frank was disgusted with the idea of going nowhere in sleazy bars. With Bertrand interested in his work, he left the group to pursue a solo career.

Choppy waters, the familiar smell of smoke, and trout frying in butter beckoned. With some stashed cash, Frank mail-ordered plans for an A-frame cabin, a cozy, easy to maintain dwelling especially suitable for harsh Quebec winters. Frank and his friend Ken Sinclair (last seen on the beaches of Grand Cayman) spent the summer of 1971 building the cabin on his Lac Tremblant property. The site was about 80 feet up, on a huge rock overlooking the lake, about three miles from the landing. Frank engineered a trolley system to transport the materials to the top of the rock. On foot, he and Ken hauled the lumber the remaining distance.

When not at Lac Tremblant, Frank enjoyed boating at home in Montreal. As a member of the Royal Saint Lawrence Yacht Club, on the shores of Lac St. Louis in Montreal, Frank sailed his "Dicke Kip" (Dutch for Chubby Chicken), an Olympic class sailboat known as a Flying Dutchman. Lac St. Louis has miles of undisturbed shorelines and pleasant little nooks and crannies that delight city-bound cruisers. After an expedition, Frank entertained the 'salts,' businessmen and amateur boating enthusiasts who gathered in the clubhouse. He played his regular round of classics, pops and his own compositions. He dated Carole Ann Nichols, the club's secretary for about a year. With few musical prospects in the offering, he proposed. With great faith in his musical abilities, Carole accepted.

They were married in May, 1971. He bought a Pontiac stationwagon they dubbed Betsy to accommodate his new family. His compact Sunbird wasn't big enough for the couple and Carole's two daughters, four-year-old Nancy and six-year-old Sandra. Lady, a golden retriever, joined the family. They all moved into a home at 25 Kilarney Gardens, in idyllic Pointe-Claire, down the street from the Yacht Club. Frank bought an upright Yamaha piano for his studio above the garage because the Heintzman grand he had bought with his pay from A.E. Lepage wouldn't fit up the stairs. The town was named after St. Joachim Church and a windmill erected on the point in 1710. Groves of maples towered in Clear Pointe Park across the street. There was a huge one in the front yard. Maples arched their way to the pier at the end of the street. At Clear Pointe Park, Nancy and Sandra played in the sand box, splashed in the wading pool and chased Lady through the lush green lawns.

But it wasn't all so idyllic. Two years earlier a bitter divorce left Carole, Sandra and Nancy in emotional turmoil and financial difficulties. Nancy readily adapted to the divorce and new dad. Sandra, however, was heartbroken. "I felt so rejected by my biological father. He had left and abandoned me. I was pretty messed up. I withdrew. I'm told I was in a clinical depression. My Dad met me at a difficult time. He had a hard time adjusting to a woman with two kids and the family environment. Mom found it hard. She had this new man in her life and two little kids. She was trying to be a mother. She struggled to divide her time between Dad and us. Dad sometimes resented that. He felt he didn't get enough attention. That came up in arguments. There was lots of yelling and stuff going on," remembers Sandra Mills.

"I really don't remember too much about it because I was only four years old. But now that I have my own kids, I realize it must have been really hard for Dad to come into this ready-made family," says Nancy Mills.

Coming from a "stiff-upper-lip, be a good kid" background, Frank found it difficult to understand Sandra's hyperactivity and her determined, strong-willed temperament. Neat and organized, Frank clashed with her chaotic and messy behavior. "When Sandra played, a cyclone hit. Toys were everywhere. I thought kids were supposed to be like me," reflects Frank.

The new father labored between the Yamaha or the Heinzman. When he wasn't writing songs, he'd scrounge up a few dollars and take a music contact out for lunch or coffee. "I've heard the piano my whole life. It was really nice to hear Dad playing. We'd be eating dinner. Dad was up in his studio plunking and sounding things out. We were careful not to bang the knife and fork together too loudly. When I was older it was a real privilege to hear, in concert, the music that I had once heard in our home. I think I have a real appreciation for piano because of that experience," reflects Sandra.

There were financial and artistic struggles and a new son to consider. Jonathan, Frank and Carole's only son was born in 1972. Days of sheer pleasure contrasted with days of excruciating pain. "It was a struggle. He was very talented. He was struggling with himself, clashing with a new family and trying to put food on the table. Money was really tight. He didn't get regular paychecks."

One day, in a trance-like state on the sofa in his studio, an idea came to Frank; "If you love me, love me, love, why did you ever leave me?" The thought reminded him of an old man who stood at the corner. When Frank lived in Mount Royal he took the 20-minute subway ride to McGill. By Morgan's department store (later named the Bay) at the corner of Union and Ste. Catherine Street, a white-haired old ragpicker, with a funny hat and peculiar clothes, pulled and squeezed the creases of his hurdy gurdy. Frank wondered why this old man braved the cold, rain, scorching heat and snow. Only a heartbroken, wounded soul could endure such torment. Years later on a trip to Montreal, Frank asked a police officer about the ragpicker who used to stand at the corner and was told he had died, leaving great wealth. The old man at the corner fit the image of "If you love me, love me, love, why did you ever leave me?" It took Frank a few days to piece together the lyrics and music for 'Love Me, Love Me, Love,' otherwise known as The Organ Grinder Song.

Standing on the corner
Passing the time away,
I thought I heard the organ grinder
Singing as he played.

He had a little monkey
With a little cup of tin
And he danced for joy
When someone put a penny in.

He sang LOVE ME, LOVE ME, LOVE
Why did you ever leave me girl
Love Me, Love Me, Love
Why did you ever go?

I couldn't help but wonder
How the old man got his song,
What a tragic tale of loneliness
How fate had done him wrong.

What ever made the old man
Want to brave the cold and rain,
And tell the world his story
Till death could ease the pain.

He sang LOVE ME, LOVE ME, LOVE
Why did you ever leave me girl
Love Me, Love Me, Love
Why did you ever go?

I went back to the corner
To hear the organ play,
A policeman said the old man died
One cold November day.

I waited for a minute
Then sadly walked away,
Though I couldn't see the old man
I'm sure I heard him say.

If you love me, love me, love
Why did you ever leave me girl
If you Love Me, Love Me, Love
Why did you ever go?

Financial struggles mixed with Frank's angry, erratic outbursts. Discontent and friction between the newlyweds spread like ink on a linen cloth. Frank realized he had married the wrong person. Despite the problems, the family headed to Lac Tremblant nearly every weekend. "In the summer, from the day school was out to the day school started, we'd be out at the lake. Dad was always there because he didn't have a nine to five job. These were the best years with the best memories. Lac Tremblant is probably my favorite place in the whole world," says Nancy.

"Standing on "White Peak," the summit of 3,750 foot Mont Tremblant in the Province of Quebec, a skier can see, stretching for miles around him, an old mountain range. Not rugged and craggy, but timeworn and softened by the erosion of centuries. He'll look north to James Bay and the Arctic and south to the villages of the Laurentian Range. He will see rolling, snow covered hills rimmed by great frozen rivers and lakes with French names like Lac Tremblant, Lac Ouimet, Lac Mercier, Lac Superieur, and Riviere Diable that circles the base of Mont Tremblant and cascades down to meet Riviere Rouge. He will see a ski village lying at the base of Ryan's Run, the wide trail that descends from the tips of his skis on the summit to the door of his pink gabled chalet on the shores of Lac Tremblant below him," write John and Frankie O'Rear in the book *The Mont Tremblant Story*. The authors further describe the wildlife of the area. "...the forests abound in fur bearing animals and game birds, and the great rivers and lakes are teeming with fish that challenge the sportiest angler. Black bear, moose, deer, wolves, fox, mink, ermine and beaver may still cross the path of those who leave the measured track and venture forth in "the bush." Grouse, game ducks and Canadian geese share the wilds with the blue heron and the loon. The country is wild even today and this is the great appeal for all who come to ski, climb, hunt, fish or rest a while on the fringe of civilization."

Sandra recounts the family times at Mont Tremblant. "We were packed like sardines into Betsy with Lady riding in the back. Lac Tremblant became my special place. Dad introduced us to that place and I was deeply touched. Because of that experience there is a passion for the outdoors I never had before. We hiked in the woods and he showed us animal droppings, pointed out game and imitated their calls. He kept a log of all the birds. I felt like I was having an experience other kids weren't having. Dad was always extremely curious. I learned that from him. It's a gift. Plus the love of outdoors. I'm extremely grateful for that. Whenever I was sad, tired, messed up, Tremblant was my place," reflects Sandra.

Most people venture to Mont Tremblant during the winter for its world famous concentration of slopes. "There is an old axiom at Mont Tremblant –

"Watch the turn of the moon for the big snow storms" – and when they come, they sometimes last for days with small, light flakes falling quickly and steadily till the ski runs lie under deep, new powder snow and the trees and mountain chalets on the summit take on a beauty that can't be told in words. March is the month for the big snows, and when the north west wind brings a change and the skies clear, the sun is high and strong and the days are long. The skiers race to the top to be the first to break trail through the wonderful, deep powder that lies before them, bright and trackless. Some find the challenge of deep snow fun but tricky and others swing through it in long smooth turns with a wake of flying powder rising up behind," write John and Frankie O'Rear.

The Mills battled the frigid temperatures, howling gusts and knee-deep drifts to get to the A-frame cabin Frank had built, some six miles from the main resort area, Mont Tremblant Village. "It was freezing cold. There was Jonathan, just a baby at the time, wrapped so tightly in all these blankets, and we were slugging it through the drifts and slush and wind and cold. Dad called it character building. He always said pain is good for the soul," remembers Sandra.

Frank and Sandra bantered over *You and Your Chainsaw*, a book describing the inner-workings of the tool. He frequently teased his daughter about working together to publish a series of 'He Man' books such as *You and Your Outboard Motor*, *You and Your Tractor*, *You and Your Drill*. The rattled and miffed young girl replied, "Oh, Dad!"

The family learned how to down-hill ski, cross-country ski, pull the ski-doo out of the slush and bail out when it was about to sink in the lake beneath them. At night, with the fire drying snow-soaked boots and hot chocolate warming chilled bones, Frank dramatically recited Robert Service's, 'The Cremation of Sam McGee.'

By this time, Frank was following up on the interest Guy Bertrand had expressed in his music. Thanks to that conversation in the restaurant bathroom, prior to leaving The Bells, Frank now had a contract with Polydor. But it was a verbal arrangement. Guy had agreed to release anything his friend brought to him. At his own expense, Frank wrote, played, arranged, wrote the musicians' parts, hired the musicians and produced his first record, *Seven of My Songs (Plus Some Others)*. 'Love Me, Love Me, Love' was the 11th cut on the album. Back then, it was an industry standard to have only 10 cuts on an album. LP records could hold only 30 minutes in the space available (CDs can hold over an hour). The record companies didn't want to pay the extra two cents over the 20 cents they were paying at the time for mechanical copyright royalties. A record producer was wise to limit the album to 10 cuts. Guy suggested that his friend should see Frank Gould at Polydor. It was Frank Gould's job to find a single that the company could use to promote the album. Gould, Polydor's artist and repertoire director, the man responsible for signing new acts, wasn't enthusiastic about Frank's record. Instrumental music is hard to promote on top 40 radio, Gould told him. "Little did I know this would be the biggest threat of my career," says Frank. At 'Love Me, Love Me, Love,' Gould's face glimmered. It passed the 10 second intro. test (a song's introduction had to be long enough for announcer plugs).

"Got any lyrics?" he asked.

"Yeah, sure," answered Frank.

"Sing 'em." When Gould heard the lyrics he handed the eager musician $400 and said, "Here, go record it." Side A of the 45 was 'Love Me, Love Me, Love.' Side B was 'The Poet and I.'

Following his father's example, Frank decided to only do business with people he liked and trusted. Everett Garrettson, Polydor's president, whom Frank regularly entertained at his home, was among Frank's growing list of friends.

Allan Katz, Polydor's promotions director, and former student at Mount Royal High School, who christened Frank "quietly cracked," set up media interviews with local television and radio personalities including Carl Banas, "The Voice of Toronto" on CKFM, the city's top rated station. Carl is the voice of the Chief Gaffer in Tetley Tea commercials – the big guy who kicks his foot to: "Tetley Tea. Better Tea Bag. Better Tea." The media personality profiled rising artists on his phone-in talk show. Frank and Carl clicked, instantly. He regularly played Frank's songs including 'The Poet and I' and 'Love Me, Love Me, Love.'

"You just had to like Frank, all that sincerity and talent. I told him to pop in whenever he was in town. We saw each other often. He made the trek on Highway 401, between Montreal and Toronto, in his battleship stationwagon. Frank was a frequent guest on my show. People really liked him and were interested in his music and what he was doing," remembers Carl Banas. Frank and Carl frequently laughed about one call. "Do you have shares in Frank Mills' company?" asked the puzzled listener.

At the time, radio stations were looking for Canadian content to meet the new Canadian Radio and Television Commission (CRTC) rules. By the end of the 1960s, several Canadians had become major international pop music stars and Canada had begun to develop an indigenous music industry with recording studios, record companies and independent producers. Despite the activity, Canadian radio stations were reluctant to play recordings by local performers unless they had received airplay in the US. They preferred to give exposure to better known groups from Britain and America. This made things difficult for Canadian movie makers, performers, visual artists, theatre and dance groups and songwriters. Canadian artists and entertainers struggled for recognition. In the late '60s, cultural and artist groups convinced the federal government to spend more money on direct grants to artists in many fields. Pop music, considered a commercial enterprise rather than an art form, was eliminated from such funding. In 1971, the CRTC, headed by Pierre Juneau, instituted the Canadian Content Rule, requiring Canadian radio stations to broadcast at least thirty percent of air time for Canadian recordings to maintain their broadcast license. Many radio station owners opposed the law, suggesting there were few high quality Canadian recordings. Canadian artist Gordon Lightfoot opposed the rules, stating they implied that Canadian records needed help and were therefore inferior. By the end of the year there were more Canadian hits on the charts than there had been during all of the '60s.

Every year Carl produced a two-hour Christmas package. One year, he did all the voices and Frank composed the music for the re-creation of Dickens' *A Christmas Carol.* Carl was narrator and Ebeneezer Scrooge. "Bah! Humbug. If I had my way, every idiot who goes about with Merry Christmas on his lips would be boiled in his own pudding and buried with a stake of holly in his heart," was his interpretation of the gruff and cynical man. He provided the haunting, hollow sound of Jacob Marley, Scrooge's partner, dead seven years. Carl also voiced Bob Cratchet, Scrooge's nephew, an assortment of charity seekers and the ghosts of Christmas past, present and future. Carole and Reed Banas assisted their father in the reading of Side Two, *Is There a Santa Claus?, Twas the Night Before Christmas* and *The Lord's Prayer*. On both sides the sounds of heavy footsteps, gusty wind, slamming doors and chiming church bells dramatized the readings. Frank's original music is a collection of despairing organs, lighthearted piano, traditional Christmas pieces and reverent hymns.

By September 1971, Frank was stunned at the success of his vocal hit. 'Love Me, Love Me, Love' had sold 50,000 copies. By the summer of 1972, it earned him his first gold record. J.J. Linden's article, 'Frank Mills, a four-year smash success,' in *RPM*, December 23, 1978 records Frank's amazement: "Mills, who considers himself basically an MOR (Middle of the Road) instrumentalist, jokingly describes his ability as a vocalist (in fact, although his range is limited, he controls it very well). He did no singing with The Bells, and they were really shocked when the first thing that came out after leaving them was 'Love Me, Love Me, Love!' They said, 'Hey, that's not a bad voice at all. Why weren't we using him as a singer?' I just wasn't interested in singing. I never have been and I probably never will. That, I suppose, is the summary of my vocal career."

Despite Frank's reluctance, the vocal album *Reflections of My Childhood* was released. The album's cover, shot at a farmer's workshop, features Frank's nephew, David, and the farmer surrounded by a chainsaw, fireplace and logs. When the album flopped, the disappointed but determined musician retreated to his studio. In autumn 1973, he wrote the first part of an untitled tinkly piano piece on the Yamaha upright. The idea for the song came from thinking about cold, Canadian winters. He wanted a happy song that provided some relief.

Royalties from 'Love Me, Love Me, Love' temporarily eased the financial pressures. Out of curiosity, Frank phoned the real estate agent listed on the 'For Sale' sign on the property two lots away from his A-frame cabin. A rustic French Canadian chateau had stood empty for about four years on that parcel. Frank laughed when the agent suggested the home's owner, Dr. Mackenzie, would take $45,000, which was $15,000 less than the asking price. A few days later the representative called back and asked Frank what he could afford. Frank never expected to hear from the fellow again when he offered $30,000. A few days later the man phoned to congratulate the new owner. "We couldn't believe it. Carole and I jumped up and down. We were so excited," remembers Frank. The A-frame cabin and lot were sold for $12,000 and the family purchased the lot which held the chateau – Frank's wilderness dream home. Dr. MacKenzie, a surgeon from Nova Scotia, built the home's Santa Claus fireplace with stones trucked in from Cape Breton Island. Mice had eaten most of the woven tapestries, on the bottom portion of this French Canadian home, built by a lumberyard dealer in 1882. Frank took down the vertical boards, numbered them, packed the wall with

Frank's View

Don't Believe the Musical Myths

Many people don't achieve high levels of musical performance. Only a handful of the thousands of young persons who begin to learn a musical instrument every year, ever become professional musicians or play in a symphony orchestra. Musical pursuits are often abandoned early. Part of the reason is that many individuals believe the myths surrounding music. Here's my opinion on the most common of those myths:

"Musicians are born." Individuals are supposed to fail in their musical efforts because they lack the special "gift." This "gift" or talent for music is supposed to set a small number of people apart from birth and destines them for musical excellence. In fact, few individuals possess the "gift" of a Mozart or a Beethoven. Rather, most people possess the characteristics needed to perform music well. The differences in achievement are often related to experience, opportunity, motivation, learning and persistence. Most professional musicians were not child prodigies. Few musicians show exceptional signs of musical ability in infancy or even after studying an instrument for some years.

"I can only play or write when inspired." This is a fallacy of the lightning stroke of genius. Many people don't dare begin because they believe there must be an ability encoded in a gene that only a few lucky folks have. Don't wait for the lightning stroke of genius. You might die first. It might not come at all. Write or play every day. Eventually you'll become good at whatever you pursue. High functioning capacity in whatever area of pursuit is learned. How? By practicing the skill, learning about the subject, and being open to trying it again and again. Do it. Live it. Talent is a combination of passion, perseverance and the familiarity with life:

T training, good instructors
A assurance, ambition
L learning, love, life
E encouragement, energy, enthusiasm, environment
N nurturing
T times being tested

"Musical ability runs in families." Sometimes but not always. Children who have not been exposed to musical opportunities in early years perform equally well

when given encouragement and appropriate opportunities.

"You either have it or you don't." In certain aspects of musical ability this may be somewhat true. In my case, I have a particular talent for melody. However, every successful musician I know (including myself) has spent many years of intense preparation and practice. Generally speaking, TECHNICAL and EXPRESSIVE are the two broad types of musical skill required to perform music.

Technical skills are all the things which allow a musician to complete an accurate performance including pitch ability, tuning, motor coordination, etc. If the interest in music was simply based on technique, then computers would easily do the job.

Expressive skills are the additions that give music its feel, voice and mood. Experienced performers suggest there is a deep personal connection in the ability to "feel" how the music goes. Demonstrative musicians play "with feeling," "from the heart," from somewhere "deep within their soul." The emotional connection to music heightens the performance. Anyone can develop technical skills through practice, hard work and persistence. Expressive skills, however, are the gifts of music. For some musicians, there is a need, drive, passion to perform and compose music that comes from deep within. I think you can enhance this natural gift. But you can't develop something you don't have. A musician who decides to continue shaping his craft is compelled to do so from the deepest realms of the mind and life.

Frank Mills

insulation and refitted the boards. He insulated, gyprocked and stuccoed the upper portion. He also added a tin roof.

At Lac Tremblant, the licks of frost turned the grass blades silvery, bees squirmed in spider's webs, the mists rose off the lake like white shimmering veils, and the loons slide across the glass lake calling out their eerie calls. A rash wind blew leaves across the landing, their dry edges whispering against stone. At night, the blankets and down comforters were piled sky-high. The huge stone fireplace shot sparkling orange, red and yellow glints. At Lac Tremblant, family, financial and marriage troubles temporarily eased. "Those were the tender and best family moments. I taught the kids how to water ski, fish, drive boats, skate. They did it all well. They were Canadian kids. I miss those days. I wish I could bring back those days with the family," Frank says with a hint of sadness.

With 'Love Me, Love Me, Love' number one in Canada, Frank was gaining some recognition. Mack David (brother of Hal David who wrote with Burt Bacharach), who composed the lyrics to such classics as 'Bibbety Boppety Boo,' wanted to release Frank's song on his US label, Sunrecords. In Los Angeles Frank and Mack discussed the US release and a songwriting collaboration. 'Love Me, Love Me, Love' didn't do that well in the US, landing at number 46 on the top 100 charts. The two men wrote 'Don't Throw it Away,' a song about a lonely, friendless, old guy who hopes someone will send him a used birthday card, 'How Can I be Sure,' 'One Summer Day,' and 'What do you Think of Love.' Mack wanted fifty percent of any earnings over the next five years. Michael Richards, former fraternity brother and now Frank's lawyer, said he didn't like the smell of the deal. Feeling the same way but unable to negotiate down to thirty percent, Frank turned down the offer.

"I'll never know how my life would have changed if I had moved to Los Angeles and written with Mack. There is a small part of me that regrets that. It may have been for the better or the worse. I'll never know," Frank wonders. Arranging and writing film scores has always been a latent interest. Frank is especially fond of John Williams, a composer, who spearheaded a tremendous revival in orchestra film scoring, a combination of pop and orchestra, beginning with his scores for *Poseidon Adventure* (1971), *The Towering Inferno* (1974), *Jaws* (1975), *Star Wars* (1977), *Close Encounters* (1977) and *Schindler's List* (1993).

In March 1974, he completed his tinkly piano piece in C *sharp*. The financial picture was worsening. Previous albums weren't selling. Royalties were dribbles. The bank account was nearly empty. The hits were fading. Guy Bertrand had left Polydor to start his own company, Sonogram Records. With borrowed money, Frank recorded *Frank Mills An Instrumental Album*, with Sonogram. His untitled tinkly piano piece was the 11th cut on the album. Days before the album was recorded, seven-year-old Nancy asked her Dad to fix her battered, well-used music box. "It was a black box, ragged and beaten up from playing it so much. There was a Chinese-looking design on the outside. When you opened it there was a plastic ballerina. She had a broken arm. Cheezy rings and stuff sat on the red velvet. I asked Dad if he could fix it because she wasn't turning," remembers Nancy.

When Frank looked at the ballerina with the broken arm he said, "That's it, the name of the song, 'Music Box Dancer.' " The album was released but didn't do well because of minimal promotional efforts and no budget. There were, however, growing signs of interest. Carl Banas played 'Music Box Dancer' on his radio program. "It was this infectious thing. I couldn't get it out of my head. We were swamped with calls. Piano teachers called to ask for the sheet music. I phoned Frank. He sent a hand-written score to the caller," remembers Carl.

John Loweth, former dee-jay at CHNL Sudbury and CFGM Toronto, record promoter and sales promotion manager for Chappell Records, was a regular listener to Carl's show. As a promoter, it was John's job to seek out promising talent, obtain the rights to produce sheet music and then sell the product. John felt he had missed several opportunities. On Saturday nights in a Sudbury bar, John had watched a raunchy cowboy belt out songs about miners, beer and bingo. "I kept seeing him play in the club just for beer. People used to hate him but paid to hear him. In the music business that tells you something," remembers John Loweth. Stompin' Tom Connors became a huge Canadian success.

John also missed the promotion opportunities for the Merrymen, a musical group from Barbados. Canadian artist, Hagood Hardy had a hit with his song, 'Homecoming,' once the background music for a Salada tea commercial. Frustrated by his day job and looking to set up his own company, John approached Hagood about obtaining the rights to 'Homecoming' for distributing sheet music. Hagood signed a contract with someone else.

John was fascinated with Frank's song 'The Poet and I,' thinking it might be another 'Homecoming.' It took John several weeks to muster up the courage, find the writer and ask him about rights for sheet music. While Frank thought it was a great idea, he had a contract with Chappell. John suggested that the pair could do better on their own, maybe even sell a million copies of sheet music. Jerry Renewych, president of Chappell, laughed when Frank told him about John's offer. Convinced they could only sell 25,000 copies, Jerry released Frank. After selling 25,000 copies he would regain the rights. "Sometimes you get this gut feeling that something is going to be a hit. That was my feeling with Frank. I thought his music had the potential for a big hit. Instrumental music was popular at the time. As it turned out, 'The Poet and I' never did make it big. 'Music Box Dancer' was the real hit," remembers John.

Sonogram went bankrupt six months after the release of Frank's album, *Frank Mills An Instrumental Album.* In financial despair, Frank was considering moving to Toronto where many of the major music companies were located. In 1979 Rene Levesque and Parti Quebecois came to power in Quebec, and instituted many changes in Quebec society that strengthened the influence of the French-speaking majority and protected its cultural identity. Frank resented the language and cultural wars where French signs replaced English signs and English schools were closed. Though sympathetic to the cause of French Canadians, Frank had always felt there were better ways of relieving their inferiority complexes.

A job kept the family in Montreal for a while longer. Wayne Grigsby (now a writer with the CBC series *North of 60*) offered Frank a job playing piano on CBC's variety show, *Sunday Brunch.* For two years, the crew rehearsed on Thursday night for Sunday's live performance. "It was a fun show and good experience. But live TV is unforgiving. It vividly exposes all your defects, from a pimple on your nose to a slight slur on the piano," Frank notes.

The royalty dribbles, earnings from *Sunday Brunch*, his job as secretary/treasurer for the Municipality of Lac Tremblant Nord and Carole's earnings kept the family surviving on about $12,000 per year. "Sunday Brunch was Kraft Dinner," remembers the musician. He also did commercials, jingles and any music productions he could find. In 1976 he won a New York Film Festival Award for his sound track "Ski East," used as a promotion piece for the state. He also recorded an album under the sponsorship of the Canadian Talent Library, composing and recording soundtracks for some film projects.

"Sometimes there'd be powdered milk and other times real milk, sometimes margarine, other times butter. He wrote some beautiful music but there were many times he almost quit. He came very close to saying 'I can't,' " reflects Sandra.

Frank locked himself in his studio and wrote. "It's done through the sheer drudgery of work. It's work and it's not marvelous. A fury comes and visits you and you write a song. You look at it and say it's crap. Chuck it. You sit there with your pen and you scratch something else out. Chuck it. You scratch something else out and maybe it's good. If it's not, you chuck it. You have mountains of paper behind you, some of it in the basket and some of it not in the basket. You're writing and chucking as fast as it's coming. This is good, this isn't. And you keep doing it. That's songwriting," says Frank. Frustrated by the interruption in his songwriting routine, he delivered Sandra's forgotten lunch. He was also annoyed at Marilyn's taps on the front door. "Mr. Mills, can you come out and play wif me?" whined the preschooler from next door.

"Everyone thought that because I was home I wasn't working. I remember being up in my studio, totally exhausted and totally frustrated and feeling like I was going nowhere. And just about ready to quit." To deal with his frustration and become involved in the music scene, Frank walked the downtown streets of Montreal. He visited shops crammed with shiny fruit, stalls loaded with carnations and newsstands buried under piles of foreign periodicals. To a struggling songwriter, the boulevards crowded with people, the smells of burnt sugar and garlic, the sounds of eclectic music in the streets provided relief from the frustrating and sometimes unfruitful creative efforts.

The Mills spent much time with the Batson family, Liz, Peter and their two children Christopher and Jennie, who lived in Toronto. While visiting pharmaceutical companies in Montreal, Peter stayed with Frank and Carole. At other times, the two families spent the weekends at Lac Tremblant. Peter remembers talks with his frustrated friend: "When I used to stay with Frank and Carole in Montreal, we had some really nice talking times. The two of us took Lady out for a walk along the lake front or to the park across the street. We were both in our late 20s, married and setting up a family. His son Jonathan and my son Christopher have remained good friends over the years. Frank was a very introspective guy. We were guys of the 50s. You weren't supposed to talk about yourself and your feelings. But Frank always had this serious side. He was always so introspective. We talked about what we were doing and the feelings we had about many things. He was concerned about music, whether he should be in or out of it. He wasn't making much money and it was really tough."

While in Toronto on business, Frank stayed with the Batsons. One evening, when Peter was out of town and Frank was a house guest, Liz received a call from the local Boy Scout group asking if she could billet a visiting lad. An hour or so later, the surprised Liz discovered a Scout leader at the front door. "I was expecting a Boy Scout but I got a man," laughs Liz Batson. Liz introduced Jack, the Scout leader, to Frank, clad in his underwear, who was in the living room watching TV. A few minutes later Peter walked in.

"Oh Hi, Frank. Who are you?" Peter asked Jack.

"Who are you?" the puzzled Jack asked Peter.

"I'm the husband," responded Peter.

"Who are you?" Jack asked Frank.

"I'm Frank." Liz and Frank dubbed the Scout leader, who thought Frank was Liz's husband Peter, "Stonehenge Jack," since he came from a town near the famous English historical site.

As Frank was considered one of the family, such incidents were normal. "He arrived with five dollars in his pocket and left with five dollars in his pocket. He always said to us, 'When I make my million dollars, I'll remember you guys.' He had the pullout couch at his house and we had the pullout couch at our house. He was part of the family. The joke between us was, 'you're the brother I never had.' Frank replied, 'you're the sister I never wanted,' " jokes Liz. Sharing a bond of dry British humor that remains intact today, Frank and Liz frequently laughed over the gormless clock which graced the kitchen wall in the Mills Pointe-Claire home.

Liz remembers seeing Frank and Carole drift apart, their conflicting personalities and their differing goals. In Liz's opinion, the Mills marriage unraveled when Carole and Frank each took a different path. "Frank's life was changing. Carole certainly supported him a great deal in the early days. Seems to me that Carole wasn't able or willing to change at the same rate as her husband." During his visits with Liz and Peter, the couple's friend expressed his growing doubts and concerns about his marriage. "Frank was ready to get out of the marriage. Their relationship was strained. Carole, with her instinctive mothering personality, nagged continually. That was the topic of conversations. Frank, on the other hand, had difficulty with the organization and routine of a family. I think that was hard for him. Then there were Frank's creating, artistic problems. Carole wasn't quite as free flowing and flexible in some activities. They were each coping with the change at a different rate and in a different way. Frank was in search of his career. Perhaps they lost touch with each other's goals. Over the years, their very different personalities were emphasized. Emotionally and physically, Carole was high maintenance. That was in conflict with a very ordinary guy, Frank."

Adding more pressure to the situation, Frank desperately tried to promote his own music. He roamed the country with Betsy stuffed with records he'd received in lieu of payment when Sonogram went broke. Desperate, he went back to Polygram. Instantly, he clicked with Michael Hoppe, the company's new artist and repertoire director. Over tuna fish sandwiches in Frank's home, the two discussed recording, music, family and whatever.

In fall 1977, hoping for better prospects, the family sold the house at Pointe-Claire, packed up Betsy and the Sunbird. Michael Richards purchased the upright Yamaha, and the Mills family moved to Toronto, with its extremes of wealth and poverty, costly housing, horrendous traffic jams, sports, theatre, film and music industry. The family bought a red brick rowhouse at 397 Wellesley Street East in Cabbagetown, a trendy neighborhood just east of the downtown area. Frank hoped the move would give him and Carole another chance at their crumbling marriage. Cabbagetown was named after poor Irish immigrants who grew cabbages in their front yards. Houses that sold in the $25,000 range just two decades ago fetch $300,000 and more today. Cabbagetown has streets of 18th and 19th-century houses, churches, hospitals, giant trees, mixed with modern houses. Throughout the area, numerous residences pay tribute to the Victorian era with sunburst patterns, carved wood, ornate gables, wrought iron cresting, barge-board trim and stained glass.

With a kite purchased with the last $15 in the food budget, Frank taught Jonathan, Sandra and Nancy the art of kite flying in nearby Riverdale Park at the end of Wellesley Street. Within the park, the family also enjoyed Riverdale Farm, a children's farm complete with farm animals, Pennsylvania German-style barn built in 1858, a light sleigh from the turn of the century, and a replica of a Conestoga wagon. "I remember raccoons in the back yard and flying kites with Dad in the park. We used to go for walks to get ice cream," recalls Jonathan Mills.

Frank eked out a living doing commercials, playing a few gigs and renovating houses. Toronto's arts, entertainment and nightlife scene was around the corner: Roy Thompson Hall; MacMillan Theatre, an important place to hear avant-garde artists and stars of the future; O'Keefe Centre, home of Canadian Opera Company, National Ballet of Canada, visiting comedians, pre-Broadway musicals, rock stars and almost anyone else who can fill it; St. Lawrence Centre for the Arts; Pantages Theatre; North York Centre for the Performing Arts; and numerous jazz, rock, rhythm and blues clubs. He walked to jingle houses, lounges, recording studios, record companies, booking agents and music companies.

Frantic to support his family, he obtained a City of Toronto cab driver's license, from Beck's Cabs, on March 22, 1978. Meanwhile, Frank was still working with Michael Hoppe. "For over a year we discussed Frank doing cover versions of existing hits like ABBA's 'Knowing Me, Knowing You,' and 'Dancing Queen.' He was arranging these various hits at his own cost. Unfortunately, after spending considerable time with him and trying to get this going, it didn't work out. I don't remember exactly why it didn't work. Maybe the arrangements weren't distinctive enough or the songs didn't have any style or something like that. At the time, much of the repertoire I was getting was from Europe, where famous instrumentalists made huge amounts of money doing cover versions of existing songs. We were trying to duplicate a successful formula. He was terribly disappointed. I told him we couldn't use the arrangements. He was at the end. I remember him telling me he was going to drive a cab. I said to him, 'I feel really bad about this. Do you have any other music I can put out?' He showed me the vocal record. 'Sorry, Chappy, we'll have to pass on that one.' 'Do you have anything else?' I asked again," remembers Michael Hoppe.

"I've got a tape in the drawer," Frank said.

"Bring it in, Chappy and we'll hav a listen," Hoppe responded. The next week, after listening to two or three pieces he said, "We've heard enough. We don't need to go through the entire album. What about your performance royalties for your best two cuts. Let's hear them."

"The best one is 'The Poet and I.' "

"A soft romantic ballad," Hoppe nodded after hearing the piece. "The other one?"

" 'Music Box Dancer.' "

"Hmmm, a little piano tinkly thing," Hoppe announced. "I tell you what, Chappy. We'll put out a disk jockey single with A side 'The Poet and I,' and B side that little tinkly thing, what you call, er, humn, hmmm ... 'Music Box Whatever.' "

"How many do you think you'll sell?" asked Frank.

"Who knows? Maybe two thousand, maybe five thousand, maybe seven thousand? There's really no way to tell," the director shrugged.

Michael shipped the 45 to radio stations across the country. On April 14, 1978, Frank got a call from Dave Watts, radio music director at CFRA Radio-Ottawa, whom Frank had met through The Bells. Frank remembers Dave Watts saying something like: "We've just had the most incredible thing happen. The switch boards have been jammed for the last two hours. I got this 45 promo. I listened to Side A and said, 'nah, we can't play that.' Because it was you, I looked at the B side and played your little tinkly piano piece."

Frank told his boss at the cab company that something personal prevented him from coming to work for a few days. Meanwhile, 'Music Box Dancer' was climbing the charts, selling 5,000 copies in three weeks. On the next phone call to his boss at Beck's Cabs, Frank quit and retired the green laminated cab license, about half the size of a recipe card, to the scrapbook, beside his welding certificate, newspaper clippings, gold record award and various family and business photographs.

"It was a flurry of activity after that. Interviews, promos, talk shows. You couldn't turn on the radio without hearing it within ten minutes. You couldn't stop it with a Mac truck," remembers Frank. The popularity of 'Music Box Dancer' quickly spread to Kingston, then Hamilton, Halifax, Edmonton and by the end of the summer was a gigantic hit right across Canada. In October 1978, it was shooting up the charts in Holland, by Christmas it was a bona fide hit in Australia, New Zealand, Japan, Germany, Mexico and other countries. Realizing they had a hit, Polydor escalated promotional efforts, with Michael Hoppe heading the push.

It was a fruitful meeting with Dick Kline, Polydor's US executive vice president. "Listen, Chappy. Kline is in from New York having dinner. He says he might release it in America. After the piano player has gone home can you come and play it for him?" asked Michael.

"I went to this cheap, dingy, 70s-type bar. There was two feet of lingering smoke. Cheap women were hanging around. At 11 p.m., after the piano player had been given his 10 bucks, I snuck in, sat down and played. It must have been some kind of Hawaiian bar. There were bulrushes around me and in front of the piano. Like Moses walking through the Red Sea, the bushes "parted" to reveal the faces of Michael and Kline," laughs Frank. Within two days of the song's release in the US, it was selling 50,000 copies a week.

Realizing the huge hit, John Loweth resigned from Chappell Records and formed the company Music Box Dancer Publications with Frank and Michael Richards. John also corrected Frank's key error so the sheet music was produced in the right key of C. "There was John, 'Frank, nobody will be able to play this in C *sharp.* We've got to change it to C,' " remembers Frank.

Within a few months Jerry Renewych presented Frank and John with a plaque for the sale of 25,000 copies of sheet music for 'Music Box Dancer.' Now in control of the sheet music distribution, John put in a print order for 50,000 with one printer, 50,000 with another printer, and 50,000 with a third. With his contacts in the music business, he used the network to distribute the sheet music throughout the country and into the US. His kitchen was piled to the ceiling with boxes of printed sheets. "I couldn't get into the refrigerator and the floor was sagging. Then we'd have to open the boxes, reseal them into packages, then address them. Then I'd take the boxes back out to the car, drive to the airport, clear customs and ship them off to the US. In a few months we were shipping sheet music in boxes of 20,000. It had to be done fast, it couldn't wait," remembers John.

Michael Hoppe orchestrated the release of the album throughout Europe and Australia. Within a few months, the instrumental greats of the day, including Roberto Delgado, The Fischer Choir, Ray Conniff, Ginette Reno, James Last, 101 Strings, The Magic Organ, Eric Robertson, Meco Monardo, Norrie Paramor and the Midland Radio Orchestra and Max Jaffa, were doing cover versions of either 'Music Box Dancer,' or 'The Poet and I.' By the end of 1978, 'Music Box Dancer' was knocking on the platinum door. On its first week on the US charts, January 27, 1979, the song landed number 84 on *Billboard's* listing, number 84 on *Cashbox's* listing and number 86 on *Record World's* listing. It was climbing – fast.

After 30 years of nickel and diming it, the dream was reality. 'Music Box Dancer' was going to the top. Frank was a "successful" songwriter. But just when Frank thought he'd found himself, he had to start all over.

4

The Four Ds

Fifteen years after his prediction at McGill – when Frank belted out licks at the fraternity – Michael Richards advised Frank to pick a tax haven from among Ireland, Bermuda, Lesser Antilles, Bahamas or the Guernsey Islands. To avoid paying 63 percent income tax, the Mills had to sever all Canadian ties, obtain residency in a tax haven and get out of the country by March 31, 1979.

Betsy sounded like she had emphysema, her steering wheel shimmied wildly at speeds over thirty-five and her oil leak tattooed the road wherever she was parked. The Mills sold the house in Cabbagetown and found a new home for Betsy. In March 1979, with Lady on top of Nancy, and Jonathan and Sandra in the back seat of the cramped, two-door Sunbird, the family drove to Ft. Lauderdale, Florida. Camped there for a day, Frank decided to take the family fishing. Frank, with a big smile on his face wondered why he was alone. Everyone was seasick. It was so rough, one lady fell and broke her leg. He caught supper – two large, tasty red snappers. A ferry ride the next day took the family to their new home in Nassau, Bahamas.

With royalties not expected for about a year, the penniless new arrival couldn't pay the hotel bill for briefly housing his family. Business partner

John Loweth helped his friend. "He was broke. Fortunately, with the sheet music selling so well, I got some cash advances to carry him over," remembers John. Frank later obtained an advance from Polydor to purchase the family home on the eastern shore of the island.

Meanwhile, the transplanted Canadian's career was quickly escalating and money problems diminished. With a rising career unmanageable by himself, Frank hired Leonard Rambeau of Balmur Ltd., as his personal manager. Leonard was Anne Murray's (one of Canada's best known singing talents) personal manager for about 25 years prior to his death in 1995. Karen Rambeau remembers when her husband signed the instant success: "I was a fan, a singer and a piano player. He was very enjoyable to listen to. When I was doing housework or baking or something, I played his music. It was uplifting and made the job much easier. When Frank approached Leonard, my husband asked me what I thought. I said, 'you have to hire him, I always do housework to Frank Mills.' Leonard started to use that. He said 'women and Frank go together. They can do their housework to him.' Over the years my tone deaf spouse always respected his talent and creative efforts. They became good friends. It went far beyond looking after a career. Leonard felt as highly about Frank as Frank did about Leonard."

In its 'New Faces to Watch' column, March 17, 1979, *Cash Box* commented on Frank's success. "He says that the success of this single has taken him 'completely' off guard. "I've always been a consistent writer, and believed that at some point in my career, my music would catch on, but I certainly wasn't prepared for it with this song at this particular time." Nonetheless, he feels that "anyone who wants to make a career for themselves in this business stands a pretty good chance of succeeding, providing they keep their head to the grindstone, knock on enough doors and produce enough product. Mills attributes the widespread appeal of 'Music Box Dancer' to the fact that "the disco craze has left a lot of upper demographic people searching for a melodic tune. The whole world loves a piano, but there hasn't been too much of that in light of disco's emergence." ....In support of his new LP, Mills has been performing selected dates in Canada with a 26-piece orchestra. He bills his live appearances as "An Evening with Frank Mills" because "even though I like to keep a low profile, I think it's important to build rapport with my audience by relating humorous anecdotes that have taken place during my career. It's sort of a Sammy Kahn type of presentation. I understand people very easily," he continues. "I know their problems – they're no different from mine. I'm more of a friend than a leader." That same day, according to *Billboard*, March 17, 1979, Downtown Radio, Belfast, Ireland listed Frank's hit as 'Music *Bow* Dancer.' (Throughout his career, people have also incorrectly referred to his song as 'Music *Bach* Dancer').

Carole, Nancy, Jonathan and Sandra set about establishing a new life. "I admired Carol for joining the clubs, keeping herself busy and becoming a 'real' Bahamian. There were times when she was alone while Frank was traveling. On the outside, things looked okay," recalls Liz. Nancy and Jonathan attended St. Andrews, a private school in Nassau. A few months later, 17-year-old Sandra returned to her friends and studies in Toronto. She stayed with the Campbell family in Toronto for about two years.

For Nancy, life on the Bahamian island was a mix of fun and turmoil. "It was a great time for a while," she recalls. "When I went there I was really innocent. By the end of it, I was partying and drinking and all that stuff. It corrupted me. It was fun and I met a lot of people. But it was also a weird time in my life."

In April 1979, gales and torrential rain pounded the floor-to-ceiling glass windows as the family sought refuge from Hurricane David. "Palm trees and coconuts were thrown around. The wind was howling. Dad and a friend were outside nailing planks on the doors and windows of the house. It was a pretty intense experience, especially for us being used to Canadian winters," recalls Jonathan. That same month, April 14, *Record World* listed 'Music Box Dancer' as number 43 on their top 100 country singles chart and number one on their top 100 singles chart. On April 21, *Cash Box* listed the song as 41 on their top 100 country singles chart and number two on their top 100 singles chart.

Moving to a tropical paradise seems akin to the television program *Fantasy Island* where people's fantasies are reality. It's dangerous to fall in love with an island. It demands your complete attention. Walk the beach. Listen to the trade winds whisper sweet things. Take off your shoes. Feel the waves puppy-kissing your ankles. Watch the sunset blaze briefly in infinite shades of red-orange-pink-purple before it rolls off the brim of the earth. The Bahamas 700-mile long archipelago stretches from Walker's Cay, Abaco in the north down to remote Inagua in the south. Its nearest neighbors are the United States to the west and Cuba and Haiti to the south. Some 300,000 people live in this nation of islands and cays (pronounced key) blessed with sunny skies, powder-white and pink-sand beaches and incredibly clear turquoise waters. The seas create a perfect playground for every imaginable water sport.

The Mills brought their own turmoil into 500 years of tradition, progress, wealth, poverty, pirates, changing culture and contrasting characters. The Bahamas were a home base for pirates, who found the country suitable because of its many islets, cays and complex shoals and channels, all of which provided adequate hiding places from which the Buccaneers dashed out to sea, attacked a Spanish treasure ship and cargo vessels and then returned with their loot. Then the colonists came. During the years of Prohibition, speedy rum runners invaded the waters between the Islands and the southwestern United States. During World War II, the Bahamas served as an air and sea waystation in the Atlantic.

Since then, the islands have found a new and flourishing role as one of the world's most favored year-round tourist playground. There is the glitzy 007 world of giant casinos, package-tour hotels and super-resort hotels of Nassau on New Providence and Freeport on Grand Bahama. Cruise ships regularly heave themselves and their thousand plus passengers back and forth from Florida.

The soul side of the Bahamas is hidden among the seven hundred other Bahamian Islands that are not New Providence or Grand Bahama. On these islands villagers cling desperately to a fading way of life and depend on the weekly mail boat to deliver tires, hot sauce, cat food, wood planks, chickens, fridge or wire fence.

On yet another side, the islands' tax free status is the main reason the Bahamas draw so much wealth. Over 90 percent of the country's business activities comes from investors, VIPs and famous faces seeking the appeal of no taxes. Nassau, the capital of the islands, is a bustling, vibrant city where colonial government buildings, ruins of 18th and 19th century castles and former slave auction markets stand beside new, high-tech office buildings. The manifestations of prosperity – trade, tourism and yachting – has brought financial benefits to the islanders. In remote locations, however, the old, traditional island ways are disappearing.

In the midst of paradise, Frank's was a strange expatriate life. Promoting the new hit was the primary concern. One week he flew to Holland to play 'Music Box Dancer' to a horse hitched to a tree. Another week he did a television show in New York. The next week he did a TV tour of Europe – 14 cities in 16 days. In 1979, life was an itinerary of radio, television, magazine and newspaper interviews, air travel, writing and producing *Sunday Morning Suite* (the follow-up album to *Music Box Dancer*), performances, guest appearances on *Mike Douglas*, *The Alan Thicke Show*, *Lifetime*, *MacLean at Large* and *That's Life*, and gold and platinum award ceremonies. "The whole world was clamoring for this guy and his song. After years of struggling he was an overnight success. 'You're a hero, you're a star.' I was flying all over the world. It was moving quickly. And there was the stardom thing. It's so stupid that we gravitate to this celebrity thing. Maybe it's the numb who think these people are exceptional. It doesn't matter who we are. We're all "people," each one born with a different deck of cards. I became very skeptical about the whole entertainment business and somewhat disgusted with it. I learned that you're only as hot as your next record and in two years you'd be semi-unknown and be back where you started, looking for another hit," says Frank.

Columnists David McGee and Barry Taylor in *Record World*, April 28, 1979, said: "FRANK WHO? Perhaps the most surprising hit in this disco-dominated year is an infectious instrumental ditty called 'Music Box Dancer' as written and performed by one Frank Mills. Formerly a number one record, and currently in the top five on the *Record World* Singles Chart, 'Music Box Dancer' – make no mistake about it – is determinedly MOR (Middle of the Road) and every bit this year's 'Love is Blue,' the 1968 instrumental hit by Paul Mauriat which is still heard in elevators the world over."

Dennis Hunt, in his article 'Frank Mills: Man with a Music Box,' published in *Los Angeles Times*, Sunday, April 29, 1979 reported on the phenomenon: "When Polydor Records first released Frank Mills' 'Music Box Dancer' last October, those who hadn't heard the single and saw it popping up on the charts probably figured it was another disco record. But this one isn't for hip-shaking. It's a cute, tinkly instrumental that sounds, appropriately, like a music box tune couched in light orchestration.

'Music Box Dancer' is a phenomenon, one of those 10,000-to-one shots that usually end up in radio station waste baskets. Instead, it ended up on enough playlists to propel it to the top of the charts. It's one of the sleepers of the '70s, ranking with the other rare, chart-topping instruments of the last quarter century, such as 'Theme From a Summer Place,' 'Love is Blue,' 'Stranger on the Shore' and 'Canadian Sunset.' "

Peter Goddard, in his article 'Canadian clobbers musical competition,' published in *Toronto Star*, May 5, 1979, noted: "Everything about Frank

Mills is comfortable: His voice, as confidential as a doctor's at bedside; his looks, all soft surfaces; and his music, romantic, slightly nostalgic, easy-listening. You'd buy a used car from him, a snowball in January, or just about anything. A St. Bernard should be so trustworthy.

"This is one nice guy. But right now he's clobbering the daylights out of the likes of Frank Zappa, The Cars, Elvis Costello, and even Cher. The Montreal-born pianist-composer's rosy, lush album, *Music Box Dancer*, is currently hustling up the record charts, knocking off a lot of biggies on the way. Better, the single of the same name is one of two or three best-selling records in North America right now. This is more than a case of a nice guy finishing first, though. He may be a newcomer to Hollywood, where he just finished taping the *Merv Griffin* and *Dinah Shore* shows, but in Canada he's been struggling and plodding and struggling through much of the '70s.

"These days, however, things are sunnier – especially in Nassau, where he recently moved after living here for two years. And busier, not only has he his records to work on, but there's all that sheet music he must score. He's working on some sheet music. The single has already sold 1.6 million copies, the album 800,000 copies – 100,000 in Canada alone – but the real cruncher is this: the sheet music version of 'Music Box Dancer' which people can play on their pianos at home, has sold more than 900,000 copies. 'You Light Up My Life,' which sold 2.5 million copies as a single, sold only 135,000 as sheet music."

Twice, Frank made it to US magazine's TOP TENS best selling singles list. On May 1, 1979 'Music Box Dancer' was number six. Two weeks later it climbed to the number one spot. The rest of the list (in descending order) was disco and rock: 'Knock on Wood,' Ami Stewart (disco); 'Tragedy,' Bee Gees (soft disco); 'What A Fool Believes,' Doobie Brothers (melodic rock); 'I Will Survive,' Gloria Gaynor (disco); 'Heart of Glass,' Blondie (punk-disco); 'Lady,' Little River Band (romantic rock); 'Da Ya Think I'm Sexy?' Rod Stewart (Rod the Rocker gets into disco); 'I Want Your Love,' Chic (disco); 'Shake Your Groove Thing,' Peaches & Herb (disco). That year, Frank barely had time to hang one award before he earned another:

* Platinum record, 'Music Box Dancer,' (single) Canada

* Platinum record, *The Poet and I* (album) Canada

* Platinum record, *The Poet and I* (album) Australia

* Gold record, *El Poeta Y Yo (The Poet and I)* (album) Mexico

* Gold record, 'Music Box Dancer' (single) US

* Gold record, *Music Box Dancer* (album) US

* Top Instrumentalist, (albums) *Cash Box* US
* Top Instrumentalist, (singles) *Cash Box* US
* Top New Instrumentalist, *Record World* US
* RPM Programmers Award, Top Group. Frank Mills Orchestra. Canada.

At Christmas, Frank had a brief respite when the Batsons celebrated the holiday with the Mills. "Frank and Carole invited the four of us to spend their first Christmas with them in Nassau. We all went fishing and then had Christmas dinner. It was a wonderful time," remembers Peter. Getting Frank's new bagpipes through customs was an adventure. Peter brought along the set Frank had ordered before he left Toronto. "I still remember the look in the Bahamian's eyes when it went through the x-ray machine. They thought it was some sort of octopus. I nearly had to take it out and play it for them to convince them it wasn't anything harmful," laughs Peter. Curious neighbors gawked as Frank gave a rousing concert from the balcony. "There was Frank on the balcony, the sea was splashing, the wind was blowing and the pipes were wailing. It was a strange sight. I don't think they had ever seen bagpipes in the Bahamas. The neighbors didn't know what to think."

While the world envied his move to the tropics, to Frank it was the start of seven years of personal turmoil and unrelenting career demands. "The move was one of the greatest dilemmas in my life, an intense source of pain. When Michael Richards phoned and said, 'You've got a problem and only you can solve it. It involves you and your family,' the idea of leaving Canada, the country I had worshipped and adored, where I chopped wood and listened to the loons at my cabin at the lake, was totally devastating. I had been brought up to work hard, be honest, be good. I had a tough time trying to get ahead. Suddenly, I had made it. I had achieved what this hard work and struggle was about. And now the government was going to take 63 percent away? Everything I had been brought up to believe in was now being denied. This is supposed to be Canada, the land of the young and free and the place where you can get ahead? I was torn by the passion I felt for the marvelous and beautiful land, and the government that was taking it away. I wouldn't have balked at 20 percent, even 30. It tore me apart. Before I left, I went on *Canada AM.* It was four or five in the morning and I can't think at that time of the day anyways, and I was almost in tears. I couldn't believe it. But I made the decision to move and I never looked back. I packed the car, the kids and left," remembers Frank.

Frank's View

How to Succeed in the Music Business

One of the questions I'm frequently asked is: "How do you make a living in the music business?" Many people I talk to have a desire to write, sing or play music full-time. They hope that a part-time interest will become profitable enough to provide a reasonable income. Many people assume this is an easy, smooth process. It's anything but that. Rather, an overnight success usually takes about 10 years. While there are a few individuals who manage to get rich quick with a hit song, most wanna-be musicians struggle, limp and crawl for many years until they've accumulated enough experience, exposure, and stamina. There are other factors such as timing, luck and industry connections. Almost every successful person I've ever met in the music business (either a performer or a songwriter) has been through the drill. It goes something like this…

Get a rudimentary understanding of music and harmony, whether self-taught or through music school. Write songs. Play at clubs, concerts, hockey games, pubs, football stadiums, weddings, graduations and grand openings. Write songs. Play anywhere you can. Get your song out there to as many people as possible.

Meanwhile, don't give up your day job. Write more songs. Get out there and circulate. Hit the clubs, hang out with other singers, songwriters, and musicians. Get known.

Hone your songwriting or performing skills. Study, memorize and then study again any book you can on your interest. Make a splash in your home town. Fast forward a few months and even years. You're still doing the clubs, pubs, etc.

By now, you ought to think about making a demo recording. Register with a performing rights society, in case you make it big. Enlist a rich uncle, a school friend, your spouse and anybody you can think of and round up $5,000. That's about what it will cost to make a digital audio tape and press a few hundred CDs. For a fee, music promotion companies will mail your new CD to radio stations across Canada and the US. You can do the research yourself if you're so inclined. Most libraries have "media directories" which list stations and music directors. You'll also want to send your CD to the Artist & Repetoire director at major recording companies. Hayward Parrott (who has engineered many of Frank's albums) says that A & R directors get about 500 such CDs each month. It's their job to listen, discard and find something that's marketable, that might sell on a large, commercial basis. The A & R director listens to your CD and chucks it. Several music directors at radio stations listen. They chuck it. Write another song. Perform at more pubs, concerts, football games. Don't give up your day job.

Do the drill again. Get some more money (if you have any friends left). Produce another demo. Send it out again. This time, a music director in Somewhere, Alabama, likes your song and plays it. He gets a few calls from listeners. They like it. Jane Smith from Lovely Times magazine wants you for next month's cover. Other stations across Canada and a few in the US have caught on. You're getting some decent airplay. Meanwhile, you've been playing at summer festivals, concerts, weddings, and still have your day job. You land an interview with a weekday talk show. People like it, judging by the phone calls.

Now it's time to try for a major record deal. After you've lined up a good lawyer, who understands the entertainment business, contact the A & R director of major record companies and pitch yourself. You've landed a deal. Now you can quit your day job. You go through the drill of producing a record. The record company takes out ads on you in trade papers, sends posters to the record stores. You're off on a promotional tour of 200 radio stations in Canada and the US. You won't see a dime for about a year, after all promo expenses are recovered from record sales. Then you're booked on a 30-day tour through Canada. You pay for the band and the manager.

By now, your second single is reaching the top of the charts and the company wants a third. You're still on the road with the band, doing all kinds of promotional gigs and you're trying to write your next hit song in hotel rooms, washrooms, Tim Hortons, in the back of vans and between interviews. You have no memory of your acceptance speech at the National Songwriters' Convention where you received an award for Most Promising Songwriter of the Year. The awards keep coming along with the interviews. You realize you've only just begun the race. Two years later, when you don't have a hit song, you're not in the game anymore. If you're lucky, you might write another one and get to repeat the drill.

Frank Mills

Meanwhile, Carole questioned her life on the island. Silently and alone, the two transplanted Canadians wrestled with the serpents of their emotions. According to Liz, there were rumors of separation. "Initially, Carole made a determined effort to create a new life. She kept that up for a while. And she did well. But things started to change too quickly for her," says Liz.

Jonathan remembers his mother's discomfort: "There were arguments. Mom was constantly upset and uncomfortable. There was nothing to do. She didn't feel like she belonged in Nassau. It was hard getting used to the heat. Dad was always getting mad about something."

Nancy remembers Lady's problems: "She was a mess. She turned into a flea bag. The heat, combined with her long hair, was really difficult for her. Her skin was covered with fleas."

While on a family outing to the beach, Frank realized his marriage was over. "I was in the water playing with Jonathan. I looked at Carole, and I knew it was over. I could see that she hated sitting on the beach, the water, the Bahamas, the whole thing. I knew then we were in deep trouble," remembers Frank. By the end of 1979, the little tinkly piano piece was still climbing the charts. On December 8, 'Peter Piper,' the song he composed for nephew Ted (originally called 'Peter Piper Goes to Church'), was number 10 on the *Billboard* top 50, adult contemporary list. *Cash Box* listed 'Music Box Dancer' as number 28 on the top 100 singles chart on December 29, 1979.

The new year brought another accolade for Frank. On February 27, 1980, at the Los Angeles Shrine Auditorium, Frank and Carole seated beside Henry Mancini, awaited the outcome of Frank's Grammy nomination for Best Pop Instrumental Performance. Other nominees for the 1979 Grammy awards (for the eligibility period October 1, 1978, to September 30, 1979) broadcast on CBS were Chuck Mangione's *An Evening of Magic*, Zubin Mehta's film score *Manhattan*, John Williams' 'Theme from Superman' and Herb Alpert's *Rise*. Grammy watchers were shocked midway through the awards as rock 'n' roll rebel leader Bob Dylan dressed in a white tuxedo performed 'Gotta Serve Somebody.' *Billboard* said the evening's best moment was "Neil Diamond and Barbara Streisand's performance of (Record of the Year nominee) 'You Don't Bring me Flowers.' " The *Herald Examiner* said Streisand stroking Diamond's cheek was the climax of the song. The awards for instrumentals were presented four hours prior to the main ceremony. Frank lost to Herb Alpert who hadn't been in the hot 100 for five years and hadn't won a

Grammy since 1966 when he snagged two for 'What now my Love.' Alpert picked up the Grammy for 'Rise,' a dance number written by Randy Badazz, Alpert's cousin. The minor hit in discos skyrocketed to number one on the singles charts when the soap opera *General Hospital* used the song to underscore some of the steamy scenes between the show's hot young couple, Luke and Laura.

On April 1, 1980, two months after the Grammy Awards, Frank and Liz attended the 1980 Juno Awards (for the voting year 1979). Burton Cummings hosted the live broadcast of Canada's equivalent to the US honors, from the Harbour Castle Convention Centre, Toronto. Carroll Baker, Burton Cummings, France Joli, Gordon Lightfoot, Max Webster, Murray McLauchlan and Frank performed. The Good Brothers earned a Juno for Best Country Group of the Year, the category over which they reigned for eight consecutive years (1977-1984). Anne Murray dominated the awards, adding four trophies to her already crowded mantelpiece as she received Junos in the categories of Album, Single, Female Vocalist and Country Female Vocalist of the Year. Ken Taylor, Ambassador to Iran, inducted Paul Anka, who was stranded in a Colorado snowstorm, into the Canadian Music Hall of Fame. It was a double-header for Frank, earning a Juno for Composer of the Year and Instrumental Artist of the Year (for 'Peter Piper').

Frank, however, felt he'd been jilted by the Canadian music industry. He believed he should have earned the award for 'Music Box Dancer.' "I was totally frustrated by the Canadian record industry. If you didn't come from Toronto, you might as well not live in Canada. It was a heartbreak for me. If you weren't in the Toronto music scene, which I wasn't because of the move, I wasn't considered part of the action. I had a lot of bones to chew with them. I never got an award for 'Music Box Dancer.' The year it went up the charts, Leona Boyd won the award for Instrumental Artist of the Year. I got the awards for 'Peter Piper.' If that wasn't Toronto, I don't know what is. To me, it was totally uncalled for and wrong. I was really upset about that. I'd sold millions of records. Boyd had never been on the charts, never sold a million records, never had a hit record. She'd never been in the top 10 in Canada, never mind 26 countries," says Frank.

A Polygram press release after the Juno Award's said: "....He was up against some heavy competition in each category, especially the latter where he won over Andre Gagnon, Hagood Hardy, Leona Boyd and others. It was a jubilant Frank who accepted the awards. The wait was long (over ten years) but judging by the expression on his face, it was worth it.

In the meantime, diplomats are not the only good will ambassadors who further the communication and understanding between nations. Musicians have continually been able to overcome language barriers which separate nations through the universal language of music. Frank is no exception. He will embark on a major tour of Japan commencing April 12 and running through April 22... He recently completed a special feature film for Air Canada, *Music of the Canadian Provinces*, which will be found on one of the in flight programming channels on all flights of over two hours' duration during the months of May and June." By this time, Leonard Rambeau and Frank put together a show for the road, with Bruce Davidson as manager and Eric Freidenberg as musical arranger and conductor.

Frank's call to Liz after the Juno Awards wasn't unexpected. "He said that he'd told Carole it was over. I got the impression that they'd just had the final words. It didn't surprise me. I was relieved that something had happened between them because the unrest had gone on for so long. He said, 'Carole is really upset. She may need you. She needs to have her friends around her right now. She's just shattered.' " says Liz. After Carole's frantic phone call a few hours later, Liz flew down immediately and spent a week with her friend. "She met me at the airport. She was a mess, a wreck. It was like she was having a breakdown. It was hard seeing her like that. She could hardly walk, she was weak and shaky. Shortly after the separation Frank was dating an American lady. A lot of people not close to the scene thought she was the reason he left. A lot of people assumed that. It made it look like 'Canadian piano player makes it big. Dumps wife for American woman.' That's not what happened. Frank was ready to get out of that marriage many years before."

Frank met Trudy Philbin, the American woman, at the Juno Awards. After touring with Trudy in Japan and picking up the country's Instrumental Artist of the Year Award, Frank lived in Nassau some of the time and with Trudy at her home in New York. Lady was sent back to Toronto and stayed with the Batsons for about a year. In June 1980, after the school term ended, Carole, Nancy and Jonathan moved back to Toronto. "At the time there was some resentment. I don't feel that way anymore. But then I felt it was very one-sided. To me it was 'Dad became a hit, he met this woman and then he dumped Mom.' Mom supported him for years while he didn't work. Dad said they'd been having problems for years. It was news to us and to Mom," says Nancy.

"Mom called me and said that it was over between her and Dad. She said he'd had an affair. I thought, 'What!' It was like a soap opera. I couldn't believe it," says Sandra. "I remember thinking about Jonathan. I felt so bad for him. He was seven years old, the same age it happened to me the first time."

Frank and Trudy, now living in Nassau, juggled Frank's divorce, Trudy's ex, visits of Trudy's two children, visits of Nancy, Jonathan and Sandra, and Frank's career demands. "Dad was trying to be a father to Jonathan but he really wasn't there much. He was flying around the world and touring. It was a very, very hard time. I was angry at him for that. It was a difficult time for all of us. I had a hard time being a teenager. My Mother was having a nervous breakdown. She was always on the verge of tears. There was always this pain in her eyes. I felt helpless. It took a couple of years to get over it. When Jonathan failed grade four I made a joke, 'just like me.' I still cry about that time in our lives," says Sandra.

On October 1, 1980, in the Regency Ballroom of Toronto's Four Seasons Hotel, Tim Harrold, president of Polygram Inc., accepted the William Harold Moon Award for Frank who was on tour in Western Canada. PROCAN's highest honor recognizes the achievements of Canadian artists who have significantly enhanced Canadian music abroad. Shortly after, Frank switched to Capitol as his recording company. Leonard thought that because he also managed Anne Murray he would have more leverage since Anne was with Capitol. "Over the long term it has been a good experience, but Polydor was more instrumentally-oriented at the time. They had James Last, Roberto Delgado and other European instrumental artists. Capitol was a more US style pop company. I have good things to say about both of them and really feel they both tried to "sell" an instrumental artist at a time when they had seen the peak of this style and would experience a decline from then on," notes Frank.

At the 11th Annual (1981) Juno Awards (for the voting year 1980), on April 2, 1981, at The O'Keefe Centre, Toronto, there was a little unrehearsed and unexpected slapstick as co-hosts Ronnie Hawkins and Carroll Baker arrived on stage in a chauffeur-driven Rolls Royce. While getting out of the car, Hawkins ripped his tuxedo pants as Baker laughed hysterically.

Performers that night included Frank, Ginette Reno, Graham Shaw and the Sincere Serenaders, Powder Blues, Ronnie Hawkins and Carroll Baker, Diane Tell, Shari Ulrich. For the second year in a row, Anne Murray was a four-time Juno winner. Her hit single 'Could I Have This Dance' shared the spotlight with Martha and the Muffins' first chart topper, 'Echo Beach.' Joni Mitchell, inducted into the Canadian Music Hall of Fame by Prime Minister Trudeau, joked about the comic spirit of the ceremonies hosted by John Candy and Andrea Martin, "Well, the Hall of Fame....Makes me feel like Boom Boom Geoffrion!" Frank earned a Juno as Instrumental Artist of the Year.

In April 1982, a Detroit pianist claimed 'Music Box Dancer' was his song. In his civil action, filed in a US federal court in Flint, Michigan, Robert B. Milne, a Detroit-area musician, demanded all royalties from Frank's platinum-selling record, $1 per printed disc and $50,000 in punitive damages. Milne said he wrote the music in October 1974, calling it 'The Ragged Music Box;' recorded it in 1978, and released it in 1979 under an obscure Detroit recording label, Jim Taylor Presents. He said the record got some local airplay, but never reached the charts. It took several years before the issue was resolved.

Barely recovering from his divorce and the lawsuit that was sending him closer to an emotional and physical collapse, Frank recorded his first Christmas special a few months after Milne's claim. Cathy Dunphy, in her *TV Guide* article 'Oh, you beautiful doll!' December 1982, described the Christmas special: "It features a music box dancer who, as the plot thickens, turns into a real live dancer. Now, who could that be? Did we hear the name of Canada's prima ballerina and lady about town and guest spots Karen Kain? We did. And she's the dancer who fulfills Mills any wish he wants. ....So, we repeat, what would Frank Mills want for Christmas? His own television special, that's what, along with his choice of guests: a 'Shirley Jones type' who is none other than the *Partridge Family* mom herself, plus her stepson David Cassidy (obviously a family package). And Barbara Eden, who doesn't show her navel but does warble 'My Favorite Things' and 'The Christmas Song.' Adding a touch of bass and class to the festivities is opera singer Robert Pilon, who guides viewers through an international segment with Mills featuring the origins of many of the songs we now associate with Christmas."

Earlier in the year, hoping to alleviate some of the stress, anxiety and Frank's fiery outbursts, he bought a 41-acre farm outside Stowe, Vermont amidst pastoral hills and valleys, red barns, quaint, covered bridges and white-steepled churches. "He's gone and done it again, he's created another beautiful place," commented Michael Hoppe.

"My homes are in secluded pastoral places. Boats take me further away. I desperately need peace and quiet. Other than restaurants, culture, and business, if I never visited another city, it is fine with me. Robert Redford summed it up in the movie *Horse Whisperer*, 'there wasn't enough room in the city for me, and there was too much room in the country for her.' I'm with him," says Frank. A horse barn and riding ring were built so Trudy could feed, breed, show and care for the Morgan horses. To continue his songwriting, Frank also purchased a black Yamaha grand piano for the home in Vermont.

In 1993, 'Music Box Dancer,' was still on the charts. On September 29, 1983, Leonard Rambeau issued the press release 'A Million-Airs for Frank Mills.' "Recently, at a Broadcast Music Inc. (BMI) luncheon in New York City, Canadian piano/instrumentalist Frank Mills was the recipient of a rare award. His recording of 'Music Box Dancer' was honored for one million logged performances in the United States. This achievement means 'Music Box Dancer' has been performed on radio in the US for at least 50,000 hours of broadcast time," wrote Leonard.

In a Detroit, Michigan courtroom, in fall 1984, the firm of Hyman, Gurman, Winkelman defended Frank's case. "That nearly destroyed me. I'd spent all my life working hard and along comes this guy claiming he'd written the song. It just wasn't true. I had done all the necessary work to register my songs. It was a gut-wrenching experience. The move, the divorce and now this. I was a mess. I just about lost it. Michael Richards was helpful in soothing my violent frustration with the American legal system which promise everyone a free trial as long as they can pay for it. In court, we explained many things to the judge, who wasn't familiar with how the music business worked. In the end, after much grief and pain, he apologized profusely saying the case should never have gone to court and the evidence was based on hearsay. He ordered Milne to pay me $10,000 in damages. But it cost me about $20,000," recalls Frank.

Wounds from the divorce were still stinging. "Mom was bitter and devastated for many years. The divorce was really messy. She couldn't eat or sleep. Dad was gone, here we were, Mom, Sandy and I concerned about seven-year-old Jonathan. The three of us were hovering over him, so concerned about him. Dad had this new woman in his life, he wanted us to be happy. It was hard to do that because Mom was so devastated, and there was Jonathan," says Nancy.

Frank says, "I was tugged at from the outside and the inside. Moving separated and distanced me from my family. It put me out of touch with the Canadian music scene. It was cumbersome to be living in Nassau and doing business around the world. Whenever I went to Toronto, I saw Jonathan. Divorce is a disaster on children. Whatever kept our parents together doesn't seem to be around anymore. It was difficult for me. It was hard to accept that I'd made a mistake. You weren't supposed to make a mistake, or even if you did, you stuck it out. It was totally against my concept of family. The divorce was like leaving Canada – gut wrenching hard! The principles of family and everything I had believed in were tugging at my soul. Leaving Jonathan in a divorce situation was hard, really tough. Trying to visit with him and maintain contact was difficult, especially knowing that he'd been devastated by the whole thing. While my kids thought Trudy and I were having a good time, I was destroyed. Leaving my marriage wasn't done without horrendous heartbreak, thought, consideration and all the things that make it so hard. I suffered enormously over that."

Later that year Frank filmed *Rocky Mountain Christmas*, his second Christmas special, which was nominated for Top Musical Variety TV Show. In a Rocky Mountain retreat in Lake Louise, Alberta, Frank, Toni Tennille, Carroll Baker, rock group Platinum Blonde, Shari Lewis and Paul Martini and Barbara Underhill entertained the television audience.

By now, things with Trudy were changing. "In the beginning he and Trudy had an intense relationship. They were inseparable. But I felt Frank was searching for something. Trudy said he was stressed out and had a short temper. She found that difficult to live with. It was a very complicated relationship with Trudy's children and Frank's children flying in and out of Nassau. That caused stress in itself," recalls Liz. Frank found Trudy's bout with cancer, the same kind Frank's mother had had 20 years earlier, especially painful. It ignited unfinished business with his mother.

In 1986, Frank filmed the television special *Frank Mills' Harvest Moon* with Rita Coolidge, John Schneider, The Spoons, Veronique Belliveau,

Robert Pilon and Pat Bullard. Frank began by playing 'Autumn Leaves' on a white baby grand piano in the middle of an Ottawa football field, and later popped up pounding the ivories on a barge down the Rideau Canal. In this special, he was dressed in Scottish attire and played the bagpipes.

While Frank wrote and produced a new album every year between the TV specials of 1982 through 1986, he was seriously thinking of leaving music. He was exhausted and bored from years of manually writing music scores – write, rewrite, scratch out, erase, write, scratch out, crumple, throw into wastebasket. Years of labor intensive music writing had drained much of his creativity. Recognizing his plight, his good friend and sound engineer Hayward Parrott suggested he ought to try an electronic pocket calculator. Frank met Hayward while producing his third album, *Sunday Morning Suite*, with Polydor. Hayward has engineered albums for Tommy Hunter, Henry Mancini, Brian Adams, Glass Tiger and Leona Boyd.

At first, the computer illiterate Frank resisted. Not familiar with computers, the mechanical device was uncharted territory. A few months later, after Frank had mastered the pocket calculator, Hayward thought Frank would enjoy writing music again with the assistance of a MIDI system. "He was ready to hang up his spurs. He was bored and frustrated at producing similar kinds of music. There wasn't anywhere for him to go with the old way. I remember telling him about the song 'Chariots of Fire' which was engineered and produced with synthesizers. 'Frank, listen to this. Here's where you ought to be going,' " remembers Hayward Parrott.

Frank was hooked. MIDI (Musical Instrument Digital Interface) is a world of synthesizers, sequencers, sound samplers, speakers, synchronization signals, cables, computers, controllers and clocks. It is a way of communicating musical happenings between machines. These melodic events are actions that a performer makes while playing a musical instrument – pressing keys, moving slider controls, setting switches and adjusting foot pedals. MIDI is like playing music on a typewriter. "It was a breath of fresh air. It opened up a whole new world I never knew existed. It took out the drudgery of composing. Now I could write a song in the morning, arrange it in the afternoon and play it in my car. I could play a note that sounded like a French horn, bassoon, clarinet, violin. It was marvelous. It put the fun back into music," says Frank. *Transitions*, his electronic new-age flavor album, released shortly after his adventure with the MIDI system, reflected a new love and creativity with music. With a disk in hand, Frank now writes songs on a computer in his studio in Nassau or in his studio in Vermont.

By Thanksgiving 1986, the part in the centre of his hair had widened, and rage replaced the sadness in his eyes and in his soul. At a family gathering in Nassau, Frank vented decades of fury. "My stress bucket was full. Abruptly, somebody dumped in another gallon. I lost control. I went bonkers. It was American Thanksgiving. I caused this terrible scene and I don't remember too much else. The next thing I knew Trudy said, 'the kids are leaving and I can't take this anymore. I'm leaving.' I took her to the airport and said, 'there's something wrong with me and I'm going to find out what it is.' "

Trudy's leaving was the fourth disaster. The other three were the move, the divorce, and the court case. Now Frank had to deal with all of them.

5

SEEKING A NEW WORLD

Within two days of Trudy's departure, Frank was in a psychiatrist's office seeking answers. In a six-month, twice-per-week marathon counseling session, he poured out his heart and soul to a loving, kind and caring gentleman. In those meetings he came to understand the indelible marks left by his parents' death and his father's anger. "I thought it was normal to dish out this abuse. My father was totally neurotic, peaking four or five times a day. I didn't know any better until the crash of 1986."

At home, the bewildered, tortured Frank looked in the mirror and questioned: "How could you possibly do this to someone you love so much?" The paradox of Frank Sr. loomed in the turmoil. In a darkened room, Frank hugged his knees against his chest and rocked himself. Years of pain rose and expanded and consumed him. Eyes tightly closed, he made no sound as the room filled with silent screaming. "Where does the hard business man go to open his soul? I still struggle with the personality cards I got. Under certain conditions the cards erupt. On the positive side, I use the energy to present a good concert. Under negative conditions, with little sleep, and being tired in the morning, I have turned into a raging idiot. It must have been very hard for Carole and Trudy to live with this."

Through it all, Frank realized he wasn't the loving, caring man he thought he was. "I was not a gentleman with Trudy at the time. I was not understanding and not overly caring. If I was any of those at the time, it was more for selfish reasons than doing something for her. In about three years all the great things we had done for each other died. When Trudy left, it forced me to look at who I was and who I had become. My father never had a chance to look at himself. In that era, you didn't do things like that. Trudy's gift was forcing me to face myself."

Frank approached life and relationships with anger and guilt. "It's like a black cloud, a concentrated storm of neurosis. It silently but deadly, forms an attitude of how you see life. I was angry that my parents were sick and died. I wanted to go swimming with my Dad. He was sick so I had to go with other people. We never did anything together. I never got the motorboat he promised me. I bought it when I turned 18 with the money he left me. Then I saw his anger all the time. All that left me an emotional wreck. I had to come to terms with who I had become because of my parents' death, and move on from there. I was the recipient of my Father's self, the good and the bad."

For a long time, Frank thought he was a silent victim. He stumbled across a television program about the anger-guilt syndrome. In the program men talked about their verbal abuse towards their wives, their "world-is-caving-in-on-me" feelings, and the pain, regret and confusion over their behavior. "The condition turns men into idiots. They appear wonderful 90 percent of the time, but then something happens. It's like a dam overflowing. Like an epileptic fit. You forgive an epileptic but you don't forgive these men."

Frank now recognizes his anger-guilt complex as a crooked wire that needs mending. "It is scarred – but healing – tissue in my brain, my life, my soul. While you can't ever remove the condition, you can learn how to deal with it and avoid certain conditions that aggravate it." Fueled by regret, advancing years and changing values, Frank has worked hard to calm the raging storm. He tries to get enough sleep and exercise, avoids loud music, rambunctious children and excessive stress.

Gaining perspective on his father's situation also helped. "My Dad was a tormented man. He had a complex personality and struggled with his own paradoxical nature. He was never in a position to analyze his own deck of cards. Here was this creative man in the dirty, cruddy tire business. He always told me he regretted not going into the candy business. With that route at least there would have been some creativity. Then he got into the drinking and partying and all that. It destroyed him. That was typical of his time. Men were stressed and dying of heart attacks at age 50."

In the spring of '87 while Frank and Trudy tried to reconcile, she lived in the house in Stowe. Frank wanted to be near her so he decided to write his next album, which had to be delivered that summer, at Michael Richard's summer house in Stowe. He called Ralph Tibbitts, the piano mover in Vermont, to move his black Yamaha grand piano from his house in Vermont to Michael Richard's house. "Too much had happened. We just couldn't make it work. There was too much damage." He called Ralph Tibbitts to move the piano back. "Do you remember where my house is?" he asked. "No, I don't but the piano does," replied Ralph. Trudy moved back to New York while Frank slowly pieced together the fragments of his life. He continued touring, he dated several other women, and sought to enjoy his homes in Vermont and Nassau.

"The lights begin to twinkle from the rocks;
The long day wanes; the slow moon climbs; the deep
Moans round with many voices.
Come, my friends.'Tis not too late to seek a newer world.
Push off, and sitting well in order smite
The sounding furrows; for my purpose holds
To sail beyond the sunset, and the baths
Of all the western stars, until I die.
It may be that the gulfs will wash us down;
It may be we shall touch the Happy Isles,
And see the great Achilles, whom we knew.
Tho' much is taken, much abides; and tho'
We are not now that strength which in old days
Moved earth and heaven, that which we are, we are, –
One equal temper of heroic hearts,
Made weak by time and fate, but strong in will
To strive, to seek, to find, and not to yield."

Alfred, Lord Tennyson, *Ulysses*

One line in that classic sea tale, one of Frank's favorite poems, is a precursor to a Bahamian cruise. The sea, fishing, sailing and cruising are among his favorite activities. To Frank, life is more than music. Rather, at times he'd much prefer to cruise the Bahamian waters, rich in the colorful history of pirates, slave auctions, cotton plantations, rum runners, lighthouses and shipwrecks.

"Frankie boy, where are we going?" asks Geoffrey Johnstone, his Bahamian sailing friend of many years.

Frank teases, "Sir Geoffrey, let's head off to Cuba. *Come my friend 'Tis not too late to seek a newer world.*" The statement applies as much to cruising as it does to his life after the crash of '86. In 1988, he dubbed his new yacht, a 37-foot Bertram Sportfish 'The Cay of Sea' and renamed his 17-foot Mako dinghy, purchased in June 1979, 'Sea Flat.' The dinghy was originally called 'Maybe Seven' in honor of Michael Hoppe who had suggested that they might sell "maybe two thousand, maybe five thousand, maybe seven thousand" of the single 'Music Box Dancer.' Thereafter, he established a routine of four months of writing and producing albums, four months of enjoying recreational activities, and four months of touring. Between ocean voyages Frank did several television specials: *Frank Mills Christmas Concert*, CTV (1988); *Concert in the Meadows*, from Stowe, Vermont, CFCF (1989); *An Evening with Frank Mills*, Halifax, ATV (1992); and *Christmas with Frank Mills*, Halifax, ATV/ASN (1994).

The sea seeps slowly into your life and washes away everything else. It slowly takes you over until the only way to experience the sea is to live it, to be on the sea every day. If you encounter the sea long enough, it becomes more than just a challenge or a sport or even your job. Sailors of all nations share this peculiar brotherhood. The Royal Nassau Sailing Club is the hub of the musician's sailing activities. As the club's commodore for 1998 - 1999 (in Bahamian lingo, commode) he currently manages the operation, ensuring the club's survival. Usually reserved for a native Bahamian, the relocated Canadian is the second non-native to hold the office. Transplanted Frank considers the appointment an honor and an act of friendship.

The club's floating parking lot is home to 'Seabreeze,' 'Oatmeal Squabble,' 'Punchy,' 'Blue,' 'Buccaneer,' 'Sloop du Jour' and 'Foreplay' and other members' sailing crafts. Screeching gulls circle above. The wood on the boats and wharfs is weathered by salt air and battering sea storms.

Frank Sr.

Frankie and Kathy after a family fishing trip.

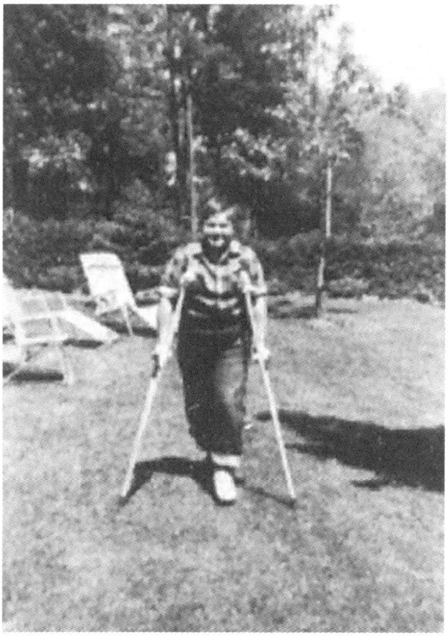

Frankie with a broken leg after trying to put chains on his Raleigh three-speed racing bike.

Frankie – the proud angler.

Frankie on the Heinzman.

Photo taken in 1974, for album cover but never used.

New York, 1979, the week 'Music Box Dancer' reached #1 on the US charts.

Frank, 1980, accepting his Juno Award.

Frank, 1979, at filming of Peter Piper video at historic Fort York in Ontario.

Juno Awards, Toronto.

Dinah Shore television show, Hollywo

Concert in the park, Ottawa.

Television show, Yokohama.

CTV Christmas special with Karen Kain.

CBC 'Rocky Mountain Christmas' with Carol Baker.

WNGE TV, Nashville.

JHK television, Tokyo.

CTV Christmas special with Barbara Eden.

Ontario Place

Television show New York with Clive Davis, Dinah Shore, Charlie Price & Frank.

Frank, 1985, between takes of CBC television special in Toronto.

Book cover is also cover for Frank's 1986 album, Transitions.

Frank performing at Great Canadian Maturity and Travel Show, Edmonton, May 1995.

Frank in 1995 with that famous piano still in view.

Frank, 1998, in his red Renegade jeep (the one with the five dollar horn mounted between the front seats).

In the Old English colonial tradition, the name of Frank's home, that he built six years ago, is "Holdin' On."

A "Highlands" sign with Macbeth tartan displays the Scottish connection.

Winners of 1994, SOCAN "Classics" Award. Back L-R: unknown; 2. Galt McDermott; 3. Gene McLellan. Front L-R: Frank; 2. Gordon Lightfoot; 3. Terry Jacks; 4. unknown; 5. Randy Bachman

The original touring band, 1980-1990 taken at Stowe, Vermont. Back L-R: Jimmy Pepperdine, drums; Eric Freidenberg, leader; John Hyde, bass; Ron Halderson, guitar; Dave Jandrisch, keyboards; Frank.

The '90s touring band on the "garlic" tour, Ontario, 1998. L-R: John Loweth (aka the Loweth Form of the Law, Lobby Gandhi, the Loweth Form of Life, Johnny Swag) road manager; Craig Bignell (aka Craigorich, Cake) percussion; (at back) Bill Girdwood (aka Willie, Bilge (because he's always burping)) technical director; Frank (aka the Captain, Uncle Frank); Mark LaLama (pronounced like a dog barking with a hairlip) keyboards; Miles Jackson (aka Milsey, Knit Face) musical director, keyboard and tuba.

Strong smells of fish mix with seaweed. In the main dining room, large windows give a magnificent view of the Northeast Providence Channel, Paradise Island and the 126-foot tall lighthouse built in 1793 by Governor Lord Dunmore. Wall cases are stacked with ribbons, trophies, faded maps, pennants, silver and gold cups and photographs. Hand-painted signs display the winners of Bacardi Cup, Dudley Gambun Cup, Junior National Championship and the Kingscup. The Board of Commodores sign dates back to 1925, when the love of the sea, friendship and camaraderie started the club. Laughter, merriment, recounting of sea adventures and jokes about "the Bahamian ways" follow a Friday or Saturday night dinner, a mid-week cruise or a racing event. In Bahamian vernacular Frank reenacts a strawmarket scene where two Big Panty Gals (robust Bahamian women) sell their goods: "Oh, chhillee, how you doin'? "

"Oh, I allllright, I tink I could make it tru annodda day God spare life, how you doin'? "

"Oh, lord chhillee, I holdin' on." The two women then count the thick stack of one-hundred dollars bills from the day's take. In the Old English colonial tradition, the name of Frank's home, that he built six years ago, is "Holdin' On."

Geoffrey Johnstone tells the story of the lighthouse: "A governor went to meet with natives on one of the Out Islands. He told the people he was there to represent them and to remedy any problems. The governor invited questions and problems from the assembled gathering. A burly, ancient character asked: 'Ya know. Dem governor come good time. Up til you dis build dem lighthouse, town was all right. Ya know. Now hard just dem fishenin'. Hey, mon. Ya know. Turn dem lights out sometime.' " (The islanders used to make a substantial living on wreckage of ships on rocks).

The evening's conversation is sprinkled with Bahamian expressions. Members poke harmless and affectionate fun at each other, the islands' people, history, traditions – a tropical paradise struggling with a fading way of life and new world problems. "First rat down the hole tail cover." (Translation: God takes care of those who take care of themselves).

"Too much sit down me pants bois up." (Translation: I've eaten so much my pants split).

"When tief tief from tief God smiles." (Translation: when a thief steals from a thief God smiles).

"Evrytin' ain' fer tell dokta." (Translation: some details can be left out).

"Loose goat don't know how tied goat feel." (said to a young man at his marriage).

"You is a bring-down to dis family – always comin' home all kerpunkie up!" (Translation: those who imbibe alcoholic beverages too freely, usually end up all 'kerpunkie up.' In this state there is a tendency to see pink elephants and to argue with those who don't share the same glorious vision).

Sailing club friends still laugh about one photo session. Crew members gathered in the dining room after the day's cruise. Mrs. Johnstone was missing. "She's on the turlet," a Bahamian staff member bellowed from across the crowded room.

It seems most everyone likes to poke fun at the Bahamians and their institutions. Herman Wouk in his book *Don't Stop the Carnival* offers a good analogy of life on a tropical island. Frank frequently refers to this book as an example of the absurdities and calamities found amidst paradise. A middle-aged New Yorker named Norman Paperman, a successful and well-known Broadway publicity agent, suddenly finds his glittering Manhattan life empty, boring, unbearable. He chucks it all to buy a hotel on the island of Amerigo, in the Caribbean Sea. Norman's efforts to cope with the bizarre characters and strange ways of the tropic island leads to explosive comic situations.

Every May, Frank and a group of sailing club members venture to the out islands, about a two-day sail from Nassau. This is a social cruise, with wives and girlfriends aboard. The grueling, strenuous, "boys' cruise" takes place in June. Crew members from a May cruise several years ago still remember Frank's concert on the pinky white, palm tree lined beach of the tiny deserted island of Little San Salvador. Boats were anchored and passengers went ashore to the island. The boys linked together some 200 feet of extension cord and Frank plugged his synthesizer into Ronnie Lightbourne's generator. "We were sipping champagne and toasting the moonlight. The water was so blue, so calm. We were the only ones on the beach. Then I played every sea song I could think of – 'The Mariner's Hymn,' 'Ebbtide,' 'Somewhere Beyond the Sea,' 'Seascapes,' 'La Mer (Debussy),' and the Chorale from Beethoven's 9th," says Frank.

For Frank, the sea is yet another symphony, a moody lady, a mirror to all who confront her. Her numerous musical selections include: grandeur in a storm, glassy surface in a calm, the deep fathoms of her abysses, her quick vicissitudes, her direful deceptions. She carries manhood to die, to be transported, to seek adventure and to become rich. There is a key of sea for all these times, happy, melancholy, sad. They tell of noble events and sorrowful partings, of the dashing spray, of living by the sea, of grim accounts of wreckage as fishermen have gone out from inlets and little harbors to cast their nets. Sailors of the high seas feared to sing of the dangers of the sea. They preferred songs about the girls left on shore or the good times they would have when they got back again. Seafarer Frank, the man of diesel engines and generators, plotting and barometers, speaks about the sea as a navigable element and an intimate companion.

There are sea sanctuaries that captivate the senses, that tempt you to linger in their tranquillity and leave you feeling peaceful. After dark, the Bahamian stars take over. On a clear night, there is an overwhelming urge to lie on your back and stare up at the sparkling sky. For the briefest possible moment, in this mere splinter of time in the warm womb of the Bahamian sky, time seems to stand still.

Living in Quebec, Frank was frequently exposed to freshwater lakes. Now it was an opportunity to sail on saltwater and watch creatures beneath the sea. "I'm as much at home on a John Deere tractor as I am on the water. The sea is not some romantic thing to me, it's part of who I am." Frank's undersea adventures are reef trips, shark dives, wreck dives and night plunges beneath the Bahamian blue green waters. Taking a bird's eye view of the area, several massive limestone plateaus sit surrounded by deep channels of ocean water. These plateaus form the base of the country, with the majority of the coral/limestone islands that we know as the Bahamas, perched on their outside edge, the product of eons of creative geological forces. Deep subsea canyons separate the plateaus. The Tongue of the Ocean is the largest and most unique of these sea trenches. Named for its tongue-like shape, it dips into the Great Bahama Bank, the largest of the limestone plateaus. Its mouth is found to the north, between New Providence to the east and Andros to the west. From there it stretches for nearly 200 miles to the southeast before reaching its terminus two-thirds of the way down the bank.

For snorkler-Frank, the outside walls of the Tongue hold the greatest attraction. Pale azure and turquoise waters give way suddenly to the cobalt blue of the depth. A sand bank gradually slopes off to depths ranging from 30 to 100 feet before abruptly and precipitously tumbling over the edge of the wall and dropping down to 6,000 feet or more. These walls are decorated with extraordinary corals and sponges. When he was younger, Frank dived nearly 40 feet to see tiny plankton, pilot whales, whale sharks, hammerhead sharks, eel, octopus, dolphins, manta rays and spotted eagle rays. He has followed sting rays fluttering along sandy floors, scurried behind schools of fish and explored sunken craters teeming with bright, tropical species. Frequently, he sees a wise old sage with a wrinkled face. Frank looks at the underwater critter. The critter looks back. Fish and human. Scale and skin. Sea and air. Unperturbed, the huge sea turtle, bonefish or grouper lingers as if deep in thought.

Coral encrusted wreckages are stranded on Bahamian reefs. Tears of Allah, Jose, Orson Wells, Theo's Wreck, Lady Moore, Frascate, Comberbach, and Bimini Barge are some of the steel hulled vessels that have remained intact for more than 100 years. Night shows off the coral reef at its best, with most of the individual polyps open and feeding, and many creatures active. These creatures are often dazzled by lights and are easily approached.

Sailing over the Bahama Banks is like a slow and low flight over the desert...except that, unlike the desert, the shallow crystal-clear water covers thousands of square miles of white sand and reef wilderness teaming with sea life. An intimidating band of shallow water protects each island's shores. Shifting sands and unpredictable currents could cause groundings that ruin the day and the cruising vessel. Yet the thrill of adventure and discovery never wanes. "If I must sail, let it be on the ocean, no matter how stormy – anything but a dull cruise on a calm lake without ever losing sight of the same insipid shores by which it is surrounded," wrote Lord Byron. To Frank, nothing compares to the thrill of uncertainty when he finds himself in the middle of the sea with not a spek of land in sight. At times like this, navigator Frank asks himself what he might do if the screens, gauges and clicking numbers suddenly disappeared. In recent years, the Global Positioning System (GPS) has reduced the trepidation factor, made it easier to sail to the out islands and nearly guarantees the way home.

Every June on the two-week "boys' cruise," Frank and some 10 fellows from the sailing club take their yachts to remote islands. On these islands, fragrant with oleander, hibiscus, frangipani, jasmine, and bougainvillea, the roads are bad, the churches are full, everyone is related, life revolves around the weekly mail boat, the tiny hotels accommodate 10 to 20 people, and the beaches are empty and extraordinary. On some islands, the weekly highlight is a game of dominoes on Saturday night. Spring and early summer are the best time for cruising. After that it gets hot, and it is dangerous to navigate through the tricky weather of hurricane season.

The yacht is a compact and ingenious arrangement for living. Home is stable without being stationery, shaped more like a fish than a box. On it, the sailors remove their daily affairs as far from the shore as they have the nerve to take them. Yet, they take all their creature comforts with them – microwave oven, toaster, air conditioning, television, radio, refrigerator, stereo, and bathroom complete with hot shower.

Macgregor Robertson, accountant, Monty Higgs, manufacturer, and Sig Pritchard, bookstore owner, join Captain Geoffrey Johnstone, a distinguished silver-haired gentleman and deputy prime minister of the Bahamans, on 'Skylarkin,' his 50-foot Bertram. Skylarkin comes from an old Bahamian expression: 'Skylarkin and Triflin.' In the Bahamas skylarkin means fooling around with me, and triflin means you're having me on. So, if you ain' skylarkin, you is triflin!

Morton Turtle (aka Mokey), who sells and repairs boats, and Neil McKinney (aka Knowledgeable Neil), who owns a chain of hardware stores, join Captain John Morley (aka The Red Whale), a short, portly, former Olympic class swimmer, aboard 'White Knight,' his 43-foot Bertram. The name is a play on the local rag paper which refers to wealthy white Bahamians as White Knights.

Joining Captain Frank on 'Cay of Sea,' his 37-foot Bertram, are Eugene (Gene) Pyfrom (aka Pife), and Gerome or Gerry Pyfrom. Sons of Captains, Chris and Andrew Higgs, Jonathan Mills, Ted Pyfrom, Geoff Andrews and other young men join the mostly middle-aged crew to handle the scrub work. A slight haze blurrs the horizon. Foam sweeps past the sides of 'Cay of Sea, 'Skylarkin,' and 'White Knight.' The land glides away, slowly fading. A few gulls scream on motionless wings over the swaying vessels. It's a wonder that the three boats, loaded with fuel, steak, desserts, pots, pop, dishes, frozen casseroles, wine, life jackets, tools and towing equally full dinghy's on 100-feet of line at the rear, stay afloat across shallow sea, open water and choppy waves.

On and off the cruise, Morley-isms easily slide off The Red Whale's tongue. Morley utters weird and toppled expressions as if they are normal, not realizing they are slanted from their original version. "You can lead a gift horse to water but he won't let you look him in the mouth." "It ain't the temperature that gets you...it's the humility." "I'll meet you up on the

Frank's View

How to Live Above the Mundane

Most of us want to be more creative. We want to invent an amazing new machine or product, direct a movie, write a hit song, paint a masterpiece, write an epic novel. We dream of running a successful business, bringing peace to the world, solving social problems or having loving and caring relationships with family and friends. It's been my experience that the only way to do this is to live a *creative* life. That means being open to new adventures, different environments, new technology, points of view, new experiences, new ideas – all the things that inspire, encourage, and move us away from a life of monotonous routine. Creativity is entertainment for the human soul. Being creative requires a combination of curiosity, openness, risk and energy:

Curiosity. Ask questions – lots of them. How does it work? Why does it have to be that way? What makes it work? Why is that so interesting? A loss of wonder often leads to a loss of ability to create. A routine, mundane, monotonous life provides very little incentive for new information, and individuals that could contribute to your next idea.

Openness. By being open you will be able to accept new insights and then incorporate them into your thinking. A closed mind hangs onto tried-and-true beliefs, shuts out, ignores, ridicules and tunes out the coincidences of life.

Taking risks. Being curious and willing also demands risk taking. Risking means being willing to leave your comfort zone, leaping into the dark, tempting the fates and venturing into the unknown, ridicule or rejection by others.

Living with passion. Without sufficient energy, both mentally and physically, ideas will not be implemented. Energy is the fuel to work and the spark of passion. Passion is what excites, inspires, and influences. Without excitement, it's difficult to complete a job. The more you love someone or something, the more energy you will have to dedicate – you become more creative.

Being an artist, musician, poet or songwriter is more than what you do. Your creativity is really who you are. The nutrients of that inventive spirit are spontaneity, nurturing, responsiveness, autonomy and open-mindedness. All of these things can help to live above the ordinary and sameness of life. Here are my suggestions on living above the mundane:

* *See the bigger picture.* While details are important, sometimes getting caught in trivialities and the "smallness" of things can rob the expressive spirit.
* *Demand more from yourself.* Considering that we only use about two percent of our brain capacity, there is much more we can be doing if we push ourselves. Demand originality, stretch yourself, take risks.
* *Develop discipline.* When discipline is imposed by others, this is control. When discipline is imposed by self, this can lead to significant accomplishments. While we all hate the word "discipline," it's essential to the creative process.
* *Trust and develop your intuitive skills.* Trust your feelings and thoughts. Be open to unpredictability and surprise. Be playful and flexible so your intuitive mind has room to maneuver and time to play while it tests and experiments with ideas.
* *Create conditions for intuition to appear.* Perceptiveness comes from exposing yourself to new experiences and new ideas. Activities like travel, reading, theatre, new people, hobbies, humor and play expose you to opportunities for serendipity and synchronicity.
* *Recognize the signs of intuition.* Intuitiveness works at its own pace and in its own way. It will be different for everyone. Intuition comes in a variety of forms including repetitive thoughts, sudden thoughts, a "nagging" feeling, images and pictures that arise from no apparent source, gut feelings, physical sensations, strong flashes of emotion related to a person or a situation, a hunch, the discovery of a new principle, making a choice about one option over another, suddenly knowing what direction to take, sensing in advance how an event will turn out.

Frank Mills

mayonnaise." "This is John Morley returning your telephone number." "He's Dutch and she's Belch." "I've got a momentous headache...every bone in my head hurts." It's Frank's job to keep a watchful eye on Morley, a somewhat excitable boater, who purchased his boat about two years ago. The Red Whale used to travel with Frank. One morning Frank found the former athlete, looking like a beached whale perched under the air conditioner. Although it's almost snowing in the morning with the air conditioner pumping throughout the night, it wasn't enough for Morley.

The June cruise is an invitation to mechanical problems. The ocean is unpredictable. It's possible to sail to the remote islands in light to moderate winds with clear blue skies and fluffy, fair-weather clouds. In a few days, there may be six-foot seas to mar the serenity of the voyage. The sea is often harsh and cold, weather conditions are changeable. The salts are at the mercy of the boat's two diesel engines, each about the size that drives a 40-foot truck. There are also the generators, fueled by diesel, that produce the boats' electricity. When you're traveling 300 miles to islands that haven't changed much since Columbus first saw them, in the middle of nowhere, it's difficult to get parts. Everyone keeps the VHF radio on channel 14. On one trip Morley was quickly becoming a speck on the horizon.

"Morley, you all right?" Frank radioed.

"It's just a small problem. You keep going and I'll call you if it's something serious," Morley replied. About ten minutes later, with Morley nowhere in sight, Frank radioed him again.

"Morley, you all right? What's the problem?"

"Er...mmmm....humm.... Mokey had to go to the bathroom. I locked the door to the salon and left the keys in the dinghy." There are hoots of laughter on the radios of the other boats.

"On this 'male bonding cruise' the motley crew of accountant, engineer, lawyer, real estate developer, songwriter and several businessmen, who all live and work within a few minutes of each other, aspires to the lowest form of life," laughs Frank. For two weeks they'll cruise .... eat .... dive..... dive... dive.... drink too much .....sleep .... and repeat the drill for most of the voyage. "It's not for the faint at heart. The spearfishing thing is like a ballet, an orchestration between two hunters closing in on the kill. We're spearfishing and diving for six and seven hours a day trying to get the freezer full for winter. You take your gulp of air and dive with your spear in hand. The fish don't usually come out and look at you, so you have to look under shoals and reefs and rocks. When you see one, you jook him. That big old grouper doesn't die easily. He swims back into the hole, a pool of blood trailing. You swim after him and if you're lucky you might get to jook him again. If not, it's back up to the top for more air. A few minutes later, 'the man in the grey flannel suit,' a shark, has picked up the trail of the blood, looking for lunch. We're outta there, fast. We don't want a close encounter of the toothy kind, so we wait in the boat until the shark is gone. Then we do it all over again. Two or three of us are doing this most of the day. It's exhausting," explains Frank.

After the day's catch, on a moonlit night on a deserted beach, Knowledgeable Neil takes his place as official raconteur. He recites 20-minute long poems about sea travel, historians and philosophy. The bond of the sea seems to hold hearts together and makes fellow salts tolerant of each other's yarns. Just as each day's fishing began as an adventure, so each day ends in the warm glow of recollected challenges and triumphs and failures, tall stories and strong drink. Between the Morley-isms, Neil's poetic spouts, and accounts of the day, there is nothing much to do in the evenings but sit on the stern or the bow, listen to the waves gently kissing the shore or the sides of the boat. In the distance, a donkey honks.

The crew has visited, dived and snorkeled around the most well known out islands: ABACOS, ANDROS, ELEUTHERA, CAT ISLAND, and EXUMA. These are the islands typically mentioned in travel brochures. For the group, the trophy is a beach where lone footprints acquire the value of gold. Frank and "the boys" enjoy sailing to hard to reach, remote islands. "We go to places most Bahamians have never heard of. Half of these islands are deserted. They are mostly raw wilderness with tiny, poverty ridden and almost-abandoned fishing settlements," says Frank. Few hardy souls brave the inconvenience of getting to these isolated islands. Many are a landscape of scrubs, stunted trees, rocky bush and marsh. Donkeys and cattle often graze beside the rutted roads that crisscross the islands. Reminders of bygone eras include ruins of Loyalist plantations built in the 18th century, petroglyphs carved by stranded sailors and artifacts from vanished Lucayan Indians and marooned sailors.

On one of these remote islands Morley added another infamous Morley-ism: "Here were are. Where the hand of man has never set foot. On a deserted island, away from civilization. And we're still here." In stitches, the crew responded: "Yeah, Morley. Another one to add to *The Book of Morley*."

In June 1996, the boys sailed to Rum Cay – another cay that time forgot – midway between San Salvador and Long Island. Rum Cay got its name from the wrecking of rum-laden sailing ships upon its shores. Before landing in Rum Cay the crew docked for the night in Samana Cay, about a day's sail to their destination. It won't be long now, Geoffrey said a few minutes after dropping anchor.

A tap, tap, tap on the side of the boat followed a 'heh, mon.' Mosquito, pastor of Chesters, the island community, pungent from six months without bathing and dressed in a ragged P.L.P. political T-shirt (the opposition party to Geoffrey's F.N.M. party) climbed aboard. Down on his knees, in a barely understandable tongue, he began his plea to Geoffrey: "Oh, how's you all white people. Lord Jesus does bring you all white people down hea to save us poor people from Chesters. Come's alls ways here fer us poor people. God bless ya, mon. Come's to save us poor people ferm justice."

"All right. On your feet," responds Geoffrey.

"Oh Lord. Sos good to see ya. You all got cigarettes?"

"No. None of us smokes."

"But ya'll does drink, eh? (with a twinkle in his eye).... pause...You all got rum?"

"Well, Mosquito. You can have a bottle of rum. What can you do for us?"

"Yous like crab?"

"Yeah, we like crab. How about a couple of crocus sacks of crabs for a bottle of rum?"

"How about one crocus sack for bottle of rum?"

"Well, all right then. You just give me a crocus sack of crabs and I'll give you a bottle of rum. Be here tomorrow morning at six or seven."

"God bless ya, mon. Crabs come morn." A few minutes later, another tap, tap, tap.

"Oh, Mosquito. What can we do for you?"

"Yous alls got something I can drink wiff rum, can't drink em straight. Yous all got diet Coke?"

"Yeah, Mosquito. What can you do for us?"

"Yous like crab?"

"Yeah, we like crab."

"Case Coke for crocus sack of crabs."

"All right. You give us two crocus sacks of crabs and we'll give you a bottle of rum and a case of Coke." The next morning Mosquito throws the loaded crocus sacks into the back of the boat and wanders off with his barter.

The crew then headed to Rum Cay where 100 inhabitants cling to a forgotten 16th century plantation existence. Cotton grows wild amidst plantation ruins. Island gentlemen, dressed in long black robes and jackets, fight the wretched mosquitoes and scorching heat. Women wear long dresses and hats on Sundays. The crew docked at Port Nelson, a small marina, along with five American tuna fishing boats. Rum Cay is a popular spot for big game fishing, especially tuna. It's every big game fisherman's dream to hook one of these feisty sea creatures. After a few beers at the local restaurant, a real sailor's bar complete with salts from everywhere and what might have been a lady of the night, the winds started to blow at 40 to 50 knots. With eight to ten feet waves, nobody was getting out of that harbor for a few days. The next day, the crew planned a lunch of white wine and crab.

Around noon the next day, the crustaceans, in their peculiar sideways scuttle – googlie eyes bouncing, claws going *click, click, click* – traversed the dock. "You couldn't put a foot anywhere on the dock without stepping on a crab," laughs Frank. "We were trapped, and so were the Americans. About a hundred crabs had escaped from the crocus sacks. Here we were, mature men hopping around like school children trying to get the crabs back into the bag. The Yanks looked at us like we were nuts. We lost a few but got most of them rounded up. We started the steam pots for lunch and invited the Yanks to join us. They couldn't get out of there fast enough."

While the crew had enough crab for lunch, they ran out of white wine. For that trip, Frank had brought the steaks while Morley had brought the white wine. When the 16 bottles quickly vanished, Morley got the ribbing: "John Morley, we've run out of wine. How could that be? That's just not the way it goes, mon." The next morning a sea plane landed, the pilot delivered four cases of white wine to the crew, then quickly left without saying anything. "It must have cost him about $1,000 a case," jokes Frank.

Many are drawn to the sea because it is a place where the elements of life are made clear by the awesome forces of nature. The art of navigation is a way to dance among those waters. In the many years Frank and "the boys" have been cruising, they've experienced many storms but few major disasters. Happy is he who, like Ulysses, has made an adventurous voyage. There is no such sea for daring voyages like the North Atlantic Ocean, Great Bahama Bank and the Tongue of the Ocean. Every year, the boys return to tell more tales, eat more fish and listen to the harmless teasing about their life on the sea.

Anglers like Frank, regardless of their dimension, color, flavor or temperament, are one of life's eternal mysteries. Awakened at 5:00 a.m. on Sunday morning, they growl. They smile when a fishing buddy's horn blasts at 6:00 a.m. They may be too exhausted to push a lawnmower over smooth grass, but they've set records wading upstream in hipboots. A fisherman might be a youngster with patched trousers, knotted string, a twisted pin or a willow stick. He could be a pencil pusher in an office with a fancy fly rod and reel, or an old salt with a chalk line and cane pole. Only an angler, like Frank, can rise early, miss meals, carouse late into the night, and then come home, rested. Forget trying to get an angler to transplant rosebushes. He'll likely be digging a foot-deep ditch before breakfast looking for earthworms. Fish scales hide under his fingernails, and a hardware store, where anything might come in handy while you're fishing, resides in his pockets – half-dead grubs, shriveled-up nightcrawlers, tangled leaders, bent hooks, wet matches, dried dough balls, rubber minnows, assorted fish tails, bottle-opener, old trip invoices, faded map, several keys, coins and an illegible, wet license. His crumpled, faded, and stained hat sports pins, hooks, and smells from years of ones that got away. The angler insists that his young son's dinnertime hands must be meticulously clean. Yet, he'll easily slouch in a boat and nibble on a sandwich with the same hands that just baited up a grungy earth creature. At the end of the day fishermen, like Frank, will proudly boast, "so the big ones got away, but at least I know where they are."

A four-door, 12-year-old white Honda and a red Renegade jeep with a five dollar *bleeep, bleeeeeep, bleeeeeeeeep* horn mounted between the front seats, reside in Frank's double garage in Nassau, below his studio. Picnic tables, a washer and dryer, a storage closet full of oil, paint and cleaning solvents, umbrella, shovels, rakes, lawnmower and flower pots are the other adornments. A stuffed sailfish and mahi mahi are proudly displayed on the walls. Frank caught the sailfish with his Uncle George. The mahi mahi was left on the wall when he bought the family's first home. An assortment of wrenches, nails, cords, screwdrivers, hammers and pliers hang neatly above his workbench. Heinz Cwzolek, who taught him everything he knows about skin-diving and spearing, gave this Captain the handpainted sign hanging amidst the tinkering-sundry which reads: "Work is only for those who don't know how to fish."

6

THE SAP BUCKET SYMPHONY

The elegant crowns of the majestic maples in Frank's sugarbush, a few minutes from Stowe, Vermont, tower some nine or ten storeys above the snow covered ground. The fingers of two adults would merely touch trying to encircle their girths. Their weather-beaten bark is reminiscent of deep folds in a grizzled grey cloth. Their presence dwarfs neighboring birches, ash and butternuts. A single hermit thrush, unseen, breaks the crisp February morning silence with a whiny *"wheeeh."* A white-throated sparrow, sporting a black and white striped crown and yellow eyebrows, delivers its distinctive song of the sugarbush – a serene and sensuous "*werreee weeeree*." An American bittern chugs *"Glump-per-lunk*!" *"Glump-per-lunk!" "Glump-per-lunk."* Tree swallows chirp and twitter and swirl and swoop. A pied-billed grebe bobs his head and hoots.

Sunlight glistens through the tops of these naked maples, warming the forest to give a special fragrance, that writer Thomas Gray called "incense breathing." Their inner workings are full of sap, ready to swell and burst. The miracle of spring is silently, secretly being prepared beneath their aged bark.

Storms have battered them, lichens colonized them, acid rain threatened them, rodents undermined them, bitter cold and tornado-force winds pounded upon them. Yet, these maples are as permanent as the Vermont hills that surround them. Every year the Queen of the Forest gives up prodigious quantities of sap.

While there are neither pews, candles or organs among these giants, Frank's sugarbush is every bit a cathedral. There are twinges of something beyond awe, beauty and pleasure in this place of grace. The delicate drips in stereo as sap trickles into metal buckets, produces a holy echo that carries for amazing distances on crisp spring mornings. This wooded orchestra plays its balm for the heart – and soul.

"Plink, plink, plink."

"Plink, plink, plink."

"Two drops to the heartbeat," is an old sugarmaker's formula for a pulse-quickening flow. As the buckets fill with the nectar, the melody of plinks becomes deeper and richer.

"Plunk, plunk, plunk."

"Pluuunnnk, pluunnnk."

"Pluuuuuukkkk, pluuuuukkkkkk, plunnnnnnnnkkkkkk."

Frank's sugarbush seems an unlikely place for a church. While God is here all year round, he makes his presence especially known every February and March. It seems a paradox. While these early days of spring seem fragile affairs of thin sunlight and tender green shoots, Frank's favorite season is the most powerful time of the year. A growth of summer emerges out of hard-frozen mud and three feet of snow. The annual tapping of the trees' juices celebrates the end of a long, frigid Vermont winter. He wades though slushy ice and knee-deep snow on nearly impassable, muddy, corduroy roads to gather nature's sweet gift. Frank waits for, savors and treasures the annual sugar moon, only a few weeks long. Native Americans dubbed the sugaring season the "sugar moon" or "maple moon," characterized by the time of freezing nights and warm days.

Making maple syrup is another of Frank's great loves besides music. Every year, he is among 2,500 Vermont sugar (syrup) makers who poke spouts into thousands of sugar maples seeking the clear liquid that is boiled into the amber-colored delicacy. The syrup is concentrated to make smooth maple spread, solid and granulated maple sugar and candy. An entire state slurps its way through maple syrup season, when maple festivals welcome visitors and sell all kinds of foods sweetened with the nectar. There is the traditional sugar-on snow concoction (called "jack wax") – warm syrup poured over crushed ice and topped with a pickle. The pickle cuts the sweetness. The days are filled with parades, crafts, races, fiddling contests, syrup-cooking contests, talent shows, displays of sugaring equipment and visits to a nearby sugarbush.

To visitors the signs of this annual frenzy may go undetected. To a Woodchuck (a native Vermonter), water cascading off rooftops, sparkling puddles and streamlets gathering everywhere and the amorous chortles of returning blackbirds, signal a wake-up call that it's time to go sugarin'. For the next few weeks, Frank and other Vermont sugarmakers will live at the whim of the thermometer, barometer and the enigmatic sap flows of the sugar maple. "To Northerners, the heralding of the crows on those first early mornings when the thermometer rises above freezing means that spring has arrived. To people around maples, it means the sap is running...the first run of the year. Get out there and tap, tap, tap. Sugarin' is the celebration and ritual of the Ides of March or whatever the weather may bring. There is deep snow in the woods. The black shingled roof, once covered with snow, streams with warmth not felt since the Indian Summer days of the previous autumn. The birds are rejoicing, the sun is warm on your back, and the promise of new life is here. Only a Northerner knows this intimately," reflects Frank.

A question is frequently asked: Why does maple sap flow? James M. Lawrence and Rux Martin, authors of the book *Sweet Maple*; *Life, Lore and Recipes From the Sugarbush*, offer an explanation of the sap-flow mystery: "The sugar maple's sap-flow mechanism starts four-to-six weeks earlier than neighboring birches, oaks and butternuts. The roots are forcing up sap through the tree to feed the branches with water and sugars stored below for the winter. As the sugar maple reacts to thawing temperatures, the uppermost and outmost twigs first thaw, then begin to freeze as night falls. Larger branches and then the trunk experience the same phenomenon, freezing from the outside back inward, pulling sap upward from the inactive areas of the tree below. The sugary solution fills the upper reaches and trunk of the tree where it freezes. Throughout the day, the sap thaws and carbon dioxide builds in the sapwood." Along comes sugarmaker Frank who drills a pinkie-finger-sized hole in the lower trunk of a maple. It's like shaking a carbonated soft drink bottle. The gas wants to escape. The drink inside fizzes when the cap is popped.

Frank knows the nuances of each of his 150 sap producing trees: how much each produces; how quickly the sap runs from each tree; where's the best place to tap; when to stop tapping; how many holes are in each tree. He gently taps a metal spout into a hole, hangs a metal bucket, and within seconds he begins to hear the "sap bucket symphony" and the rhythmic plink of sap hitting the bare bottoms of metal buckets. Even after ten years in the sugarbush Frank is amazed that on a good day, a single hole less than a half-inch in diameter produces about 200 drops of sap per minute. The Ojibway Indians called the sugar maple the Sheesheegummawis ("sap flows fast").

Not surprisingly, Frank also has sap running in his veins. He tapped his first sugar maple at about eight or nine years old, when he discovered that maple syrup came from the sap of maples growing along Chester Avenue in Montreal's Mount Royal. He spotted a box of metal sap spouts and several stacks of spanking new buckets at the local hardware store. He knocked on the neighbors' doors and politely asked for permission to tap their trees. Then he set out with a dozen sap spouts to tap the numerous maples that lined the street. After gathering several buckets of sap, he turned the kitchen into a little taste of Quebec. He boiled down the sap on the kitchen stove, creating so much steam that it removed the wallpaper. Worse yet, the sticky humidity settled on all things horizontal and was difficult to clean. The experience, however, provided him with a memorable moment, a unforgettable sense of accomplishment.

Frank bought the 41-acre farm in Vermont with 11-acres of sugarbush in 1982. Until a few years ago, he gathered sap by hand. A well-used and fondly remembered wooden yoke hanging in Frank's new sugarhouse pays homage to that era. The yoke fit over his shoulders and had hangers on each side for buckets. Over bare, frozen ground, slogging through heavy snow or sucking mud, he'd walk from tree to tree, and empty the sap into the buckets. This was a real test of stamina and character (and a whole lot of devotion) as a 16-quart bucket of sap, when full, weighs over 30 pounds. Then he took the sap to his lean-to, a galvanized sheet roof on four posts. The arch (fire box) was made of cement blocks. The boiling and finishing pans were also galvanized. He'd pour the sap into an evaporator and boil down the sap.

These days, Frank no longer gathers sap by hand. He "breaks out" a trail through the snow at the beginning of the season with his John Deere tractor. Attached to the tractor is a trailer upon which he places a holding tank. He'll drive from tree to tree, and pour the sap into the tank. A mature maple with two taps yields about six gallons of sap per day. A single gallon of syrup requires 30 to 50 gallons of sap. He'll collect some 400 buckets to make 12 gallons of syrup.

Being a tinkerer and a builder, Frank decided to make his sugar-making efforts more fun and less drudgery. Instead of the lean-to, he wanted a permanent place to make syrup – a sugarhouse. After reading copious books about maple syrup production, Frank built his own building in September 1996. It took him about a week to build the 12' x 12' mostly recycled building, with a 6' x 12' woodshed attached to the side. Ted MacKay, Frank's good friend, sugarhouse expert and neighbor, advised him to use two flat rocks to place under the foundation wooden joists at the four corners of the house and the other four points. This has kept the main beams high and dry. The upright posts are recycled 8' x 8's from the old riding ring (erected for the Morgan horses) and the other timbers were from the 2' x 8' stringers which formed the horizontals of the riding ring. Frank only used new wood for the spruce 1' x 12's for the board and batten siding to make it look sugary. This overbuilt sugar shack will be there long after Frank.

J.R. (Jean-Remi Bourget), a guest at the farm, and Frank still laugh about the "maudit cupola." As Frank and J.R. tried to raise the cupola to its position over the steam-vent hole in the sugarhouse roof, it slipped on top of them. (A cupola is the raised section of the roof that, when opened, allows steam to escape). They were out of screaming distance, unable to move, legs flailing, bottoms up and laughing hysterically. Eventually, Frank propped up the cupola with his back and J.R. put a piece of wood under it and they continued on. It was also J.R. who bought Frank an essential truck accessory, a "car freshener" bikini clad girl on a rope. "You can't drive a truck without a deodorant girl," teased J.R.

Late into the night Frank's sugarhouse belches pure white steam tinged with the aroma of a hardwood fire hundreds of feet into the air. The fire roars in the firebox. Sap jumps in the evaporator. His wood-fired inferno, the firebox or arch, under the evaporator, must be kept roaring if the day's sap harvest is to be finished in good time. He'll burn about half a full cord of wood in a season. Frank's sugarmaker's skills are put to the test. He'll get a crop of liquid gold or a burnt, sickening disaster. The sap flows through the channels of the steaming pans, its boiling characteristics changing subtly as it goes. Too much cooking time, and it starts to caramelize and produces a darker, lower grade syrup. Despite a few burnt pans he faithfully and joyfully boils the sap each year. "If you haven't burnt a pan, you haven't sugared!" insists Frank.

It takes a concentrated effort to avoid an overcooked brew. The other side of Frank, as sugarmaker, with his sense of calm and alert mind, juggles numerous mental and physical tasks during the boiling process: How's the weather? Is the fire hot enough? Do I have enough wood? Do I have enough bottles for my syrup? Have I run out of coffee? Are the buckets full for another round? Michael Richards, neighbors Paul Spera, John Peacock, and the Clark family, the former owners of the farm, enjoy helping with the gathering. There is beer for the workers, doughnuts dipped in boiling syrup for the treaters and sour pickles for those who have had too much syrup.

Frank watches for changes in the boiling pattern and development of color as the syrup stage nears. He'll skim the foam that appears from the boiling sap. The scum is usually a bright white in the early part of the season. As the season ends it becomes yellow and darkens. The sap is done when the hot syrup starts to "apron" or drop in a sticky sheet from his scoop. Frank will use his experienced eye to watch boiling patterns, "aproning," and a thermometer and hydrometer to get the correct density reading of the syrup. If the syrup is too thin, it may end up spoiling. If the syrup is too thick, it may form sugar crystals when it cools and sits in storage. The gathered sap becomes syrup in about an hour.

Over the years, this self-taught sugarmaker learned a set of skills and some sugarmaking proverbs:

" 'The first run is the sweetest.'

'The more I sugar the more I realize I have to learn about it.'

'Out of the strong came forth sweetness (I liken this to the Biblical account of Samson's gentle nature: the strength of the maple and its sweet sap.)'

'You can't always tell by the looks of a toad how far he can jump.' Translation: there is a sense of respect and admiration for the living tree that makes it possible."

The syrup is filtered, then bottled while hot to prevent mold and loss of color and flavor. Pure maple syrup is graded on color, clarity, and flavor according to specific government standards. Grade A, the premium quality grade, has good color and clarity and a characteristic maple flavor. It is somewhat more delicate than the darker, stronger flavored Grade B, preferred by most Vermonters. Within the grade, there are color variations ranging from light amber to medium to dark. Frank usually makes Grade B. With the early run he aspires to make some Grade A medium.

Throughout the year his fortunate friends enjoy his labor of love on baked beans, cereals, salad dressings, puddings, pastries and barbecue sauces. Frank's creation of "breakfast by bagpipe" is a tradition. He'll cook up a batch of golden brown pancakes. Guests smother them with the smooth, silky syrup. The smell of fresh coffee brewing lingers. The sun rises on the Vermont hills to the accompaniment of 'Pibroch,' 'Two Jigs,' 'Drum Fanfare,' 'Waltzes,' 'Marches' and '9/8 Marches' of the Skirl O' The Pipes, Dysart & Dundonald Pipe Band. Ron Halderson, former guitar player in Frank's band, once said of a massed band of pipers, "here come the oatmeal savages and their agony bags." Perhaps that description comes from the instrument's origins, as outlined by Niall MacVurich, a descendant of Lachlan Mor MacVurich, the composer of the last *brosnachadh* or "incitement to battle" declaimed to the clans before the Battle of Harlaw. His poem *Seanachas Sloinnidh na Pioba bho thus* is a satirical account of the pipe's pedigree from the beginning:

"1. An overblown pig's bladder, grunt, grunt! The (pipe's) first bag, which was not sweet, came from the beginning of the Flood.

2. For a while it was made of a pig's bladder, blown up by every cheek; afterwards it was made of an old wether's hide, harsh and buzzing.

3. The bagpipe at that time had only a chanter and one opening, and a piece of wood which would make the fundamental, called the 'sumaire.'

4. A while after that, a crude invention was extended and three poles grew on the bagpipe, one of them long, trailing and unwieldy, with a harsh deep buzzing sound.

5. When the buzzing had been brought under control, and the reed entirely, the contraption spread like that, squealing and grunting.

6. John MacArthur's screeching bagpipe is like a diseased heron, full of spittle, long limbed and noisy, with an infected chest like that of a grey curlew.

7. Of the world's music Donald's pipe is a broken down outfit, offensive to a multitude, sending forth its slaver through its rotten bag; it was a most disgusting filthy deluge."

To Frank, Vermont nearly qualifies as the lower Highlands of Scotland – mountain, moor, glen and flood, spouting, trickling rivers and shallows, abounding waterfalls, wild moorlands, hills and crags that look enormous in the strange light, and valleys that are mysterious and silent. Vermont, like Scotland, is about "shielings in the glen," "marching through the heather," "wee bonnie lasses," and "a dram or two." To Scotland's most notable characters, Sir Walter Scott, and Frank's favorite, Mary Queen of Scots, the Highlands are a place of visions and enchantment, peopled by brutal, independent folk who had challenged the legions of Rome and the terror of the Vikings, imposing a heroic concept of themselves on neighbors and enemies, while in gentler times yielding a remote honor of style to those who cared to venture among them. A "Highlands" sign with Macbeth tartan, off Frank's driveway, displays the Scottish connection. "Being a Canadian, I am part English and Irish and Scottish and whatever else. I seem to gravitate to whatever Scot I can find in my heritage. I relate to the Scots and all that goes with them. When I discovered my grandmother was a Macbeth, I found something to cling to..some root to work with. I love the wildness of Scotland, the bloody history, their stamina, bravery and among all this their sensitivity and sentiment. I am delighted to report that my third grandson is Alistair Macbeth Ball, whom I have affectionately dubbed 'the wee savage.' "

When the ferns appear in the forest floor, weeds poke through the snow and wink in the sunshine like cut crystal, the muted light comes through the blankets of buds and the spring peepers sing, the frog run begins. This is the last sap run of the season. Making sap now means bitter syrup. The frenzy of sugarin' is over almost as soon as it began. The billows of steam erupting from Frank's sugarhouse saluting the arrival of spring quickly fade, as does the pleasant fragrance of boiling sap.

While Frank takes great pride and satisfaction in going from sap, to tap, to syrup, Vermont is more than maple syrup. There is a deep place inside Frank where his real life flows. Much like an underground river in a parched land, it ebbs, regardless of outside appearances. In part, he says, that comes from the demanding, unrelentless, soul-less music business. It's unnerving but unavoidable publicness requires solitude. In Vermont, his favorite time of the day is 6:30 to 7:30 p.m. on his deck watching the sun set over the woolly green mountains hugging the valley. Across the valley is the Trapp Family Lodge. The Sound of Music family settled here after their escape from Nazi-overrun Austria. As evening falls the wind drops and every sound becomes clear and sharp. A gopher chatters, annoyed that his space is invaded. A beetle clicks on the deck boards. The metal wind chimes sway and tinkle softly in the light evening breeze. The moths kiss the deck light. A pair of ducks glide over the surface of the trout pond, leaving a trail of satin ripples. A white-tail deer and her fawn feed some 30 feet away from the pond's edge. Insects rest under blades of spear grass and cool red stones. Bird music, one song so different from the other, add an uncanny order to this Vermont symphony. Yellow, gold, orange, red, sometimes halftones of pink and mauve, wash the Vermont sky. The shadows cast by the sawtooth mountains creep down the valley. A glacier-carved gorge called Smuggler's Notch provides the auditorium for an encounter with the Old Man of the Mountains. This 40-foot-high natural profile jutting out from the cliff face commands as much respect today as it did when the Indians called it the Great Spirit.

It is another world here, where pain, stress, showbiz hassles, regrets, and fears for the future might be worked out physically, in making maple syrup, planting flowers, painting the deck, driving the truck across quaint 100-year-old covered bridges in the Vermont hills, rolling Cuban cigars, fixing the wheels on the trailer or fly fishing in a cold Vermont stream. Sorrow and rage and bewilderment might be worked out in the sky and hills, grass and wind, in the song of the meadowlark, the nightly cries of the coyotes, in the mystery of the changing light and the moon and stars. At the end of the day in the wash of Vermont golden light, blemishes fade and disappear in the evening silence when few noises are made by humans and their machines. "I think it's the effect of nature on my soul, my emotions. The spacious views, sunsets, sunrises, an unobstructed view of the moon and the stars. It's a peace I crave."

Frank's life in Vermont is a combination of working, visiting, relaxing and writing songs in the attic converted into his studio. He'll attend to woodlot management. He will cut out trees that are too close to sap producing gems. Since a good sugar maple needs a full crown, it is important to thin the forest. Frank and Michael Richards select these trees, fell them (once right on Frank's pick-up truck) and chop them for firewood. The partners are skilled at directing a falling tree by a practice called hingeing, a way of changing the fall by the size of the cut at opposite sides of the tree.

Vermont mountain man, Warren Earl, a farmer and builder of fish ponds, with permanent wrinkles along the margins of his jaw, usually attired in jeans and red braces (the Vermont term for suspenders) checks Frank's trout ponds. Over a few beers he'll tell him the latest news around Stowe. Later in the week "Woodchuck" Don Clark, the plumber and handyman, updates "Flatlander" Frank on maintenance matters. At the Grand Union (the grocery store) friends and neighbors eagerly update him on the town hall meeting, education council and tourism forecast. On the way home he stops to purchase eggs. Once, in a lifetime of doing business, the poultry farmer was robbed for trusting residents to make their own change at the unattended cash box perched between hay bails, buckets, calico cats, feed sacks and farm implements. "I know who it was, and they needed the cash," grunts Lester Adams. Red barns, slender white church spires, dairy farms, many-generation maple syrup farms and about 100 covered bridges are scattered throughout Vermont's landscape of pastoral hills and valleys. Vermonters share a strong sense of community. Woodchucks respect the ideas of thrift, parsimony, Sunday supper, and adhere to the old ways. They chop, dig, tend their animals, tap maples, talk about frostbite and thermal underwear and measure time in dirt roads and mud.

Joking about the Woodchucks and their accent is fodder for Frank. The trademarks of the accent include: broad "a" and "e" sounds, making calf sound more like "caaf" and there like "thair"; dropping of the post-vocalic "r" making farmer sound more like "farm-uh"; and the swallowing of "t" sounds, making bottle and Milton sound more like "baht-ul" and "Milt-uhn." The Vermont dialect, like other New England accents, also can be identified by a tendency to add "r" to words like idea, making it into "idee-er." Vermonters also drag out one-syllable words such as that into "thay-at," pond into "po-on-nd," and bath into "baahth." And of course, there are many jokes about Vermonters and their antiquated ways.

Feedin' the Caows

One Sunday, the pastor of a small rural church was sick. A young preacher was asked to give the Sunday sermon in his absence. His congregation that day was one grizzled old farmer.

"Should I preach today?" the preacher asked the farmer.

"I tell ya, preacher. If I take a load o'hay up th' pasture t'feed the caows n' only one shows up, I still feed 'er," said the farmer.

"Yes," said the preacher. He delivered his best hellfire and brimstone message. "What did you think of my message?" he asked the farmer on the way out of church that morning.

"I tell ya, preacher. If I take a load o'hay up th' pasture t'fee the caows n' only one showd up, I feed 'er, but she don't get th' whole dang load!"

What's in a name?

A few years back, Montpeculiar highway folks wanted to name everything (Montpelier is Vermont's capital, often dubbed Montpeculiar). They asked Old Harold what people called that narrow waterway that ran under the road from his farm.

"As far as I 'member, called it 'the crick,' " said Harold.

The highway folks came back, cementin' in a signpost, an' puttin' up a sign readin' "Crick Creek."

Harold, not quite sure of what to make of this namin' thing, said "Shoulda been t'other way round."

Forecasting the weather

The old farmers sitting on the front porch are reliable weathermen. They can tell you the weather by using the New England weathervane, dependable modern equipment. If it's dry, it's a nice sunny day. If it's wet, it's raining. If it's hanging straight down, there is no wind. If it's horizontal, it's windy. If it's frozen, it's winter. Every farmer has a New England weathervane – a tattered piece of rope – hanging in his barn.

Not to be outdone, the Woodchucks tease Frank about being a Flatlander. "Understand that we at Virtual Vermont do live here in Vermont, and in general have done so for a long time. Some of us are native, others are transplants. Note that simply being born in Vermont does not make you a native (Just 'cause the cat has her kittens in the oven doesn't make 'em biscuits): to be blessed, one must be second generation born in Vermont (third, depending on whom you're talking to). A Transplant, on the other hand, is a non-native who decided to stay long enough ago that roots are firmly established (a Transplant's grandchildren will be called Native, if everyone follows the rules). Anybody "just visiting," no matter how often you do it, is a "Flatlander," " notes Virtual Vermont, a site on the Internet.

Come winter, car ski racks mark the transformation of the pastoral community of Stowe into a skiers' haven. Stowe is home to Vermont's highest peak, Mount Mansfield, which rises 4,393 feet above sea level. Billed as the "Ski Capital of New England," skiers of all ages are drawn to the mountain's diverse terrain. In summer, hikers are attracted to the mountain's many trails and to the 260-mile long trail that runs along the ridgeline. Other people prefer the lower elevations and the award-winning Stowe Recreation Path, a 5.5-mile paved trail.

Vermont is a also a favorite Mills family gathering place where Frank, Jonathan, Sandra, Nancy and Nancy's husband John, their three sons, Julian, Benjamin and Alistar Macbeth, join to celebrate Christmas, Easter or Thanksgiving.

Frank especially enjoys the maple's four faces: manic springs, sensual summer highs, haunting autumns and harsh, unforgiving winters. In the fall, the maples' colorful display of foliage is one of North America's unmistakable hallmarks. The sugar maples' characteristic brilliant yellow, red, purple and orange autumn colors draw millions to view the three-week spectacle. The sea of color surges south at a rate of 40 miles per day at the height of the fall season, from Canada down through the Carolinas. In Vermont, white churches and clapboard houses are framed by red and gold maples lining the village greens. Homemade apple pies, pumpkin pies, fresh apple cider, jars of honey, jams, and jellies stand proudly beside multi-hued quilts, sweaters and pottery at country fairs held in churches, community halls and craft shops. The front porch is graced with a toothsome, orange-headed farmer in checked shirt and bluejean overalls, planted deep in his rocking chair. He stares down one of the dirt side roads as a "leaf-peeper" rolls down the window and asks for directions. He responds with the Vermonter peculiar breed of logic, "Well, sir. If yous was headin' for there, I wouldn't be startin' from here." That might be followed by a wink and a grin and the question: "So, why do you think you've gotten yourself lost just 'cause you've gotten yourself here?"

In such a compression of emotions, from the heights of a perfect Indian Summer day to the depths of colorless, leafless, foreboding November, fall in Vermont never fails to be a time for rejuvenation and personal reflection. In 1998, Frank's sugarin' efforts were disappointing. He collected the sap, only to have it spill on the hillside on the way back to his sugar shack. A manufacturer's defect: the wheel base on the trailer wasn't wide enough to support the sloshing cargo. Wendall Mansfield, the local small engine repair man and chief of Stowe's volunteer fire department for the past 20 years, extended the trailer base. To Frank, picking up the repaired piece was like getting a mink coat. Too excited to change into his farmer garb of flannel checkered shirt, jeans and workboots, he raced to the barn, greased the tractor wheels and mounted the new extension. "It fit like a glove!" exclaims Frank.

"1998 was a bad sugarin' season. I missed it because of the spring tour. I didn't get to the sugarbush in time. Much of the sap I managed to gather spilled. If I was 75 years old, I might get mad about that. But I know there will be other seasons and more sap to collect. I've still got 20 more years in the sugarbush."

7

THE ART OF THE ROAD

A golden Alberta sunrise is the backdrop to six abandoned electric *ranges* roosting in the corner of Maitland's field, off Highway 16, about five kilometers east of Spruce Grove. The faded avocado green, Baycrest automatic self clean sports a red hand painted 'Free Range Chicken' sign.

A wooden Lone Ranger, clothed in white cowboy hat, black mask, red scarf and blue shirt is perched upon the unidentified range beside the Baycrest. While the cold, snow and wind have erased all traces of the stove's identity, the four burner markings are etched into its white ceramic cooktop.

A no-turn, speed broil white Westinghouse rests beside the unidentified range. The oven door is torn from its slot and lodged in front of the open oven. Burners, wires and assorted stove parts are spewed inside the crusty oven. The hand painted, sun blistered sign with faded scarlet letters on top of the Westinghouse reads 'Open Range.'

A white and blue birdhouse, with a crumpled, rusted coat hanger TV antenna, nearly covers the top of the white Kenmore beside the

Westinghouse. The birdhouse's roof, door and window trim match the blue 'Home on the Range' sign on top of the range.

A golfer made from wire, plastic tubing and metal, sporting a baseball cap and sunglasses, takes aim from atop the white Findley automatic beside the Kenmore. Golf balls replace the knobs on the range's dials. The black letters on the hand marked sign, between pink Pinnacle 4, pink Top Flite 3, white Ultra 2 and cream Titleist 2 golf balls, read 'Driving Range.'

An 'Out Of' sign is the oven door for the lone yellow General Electric about 10 paces from the Findley.

Around 7:15 p.m. the same day, in the dressing room of Horizon Stage, about five minutes from the six *ranges*, Frank irons his black dress pants. When the wrinkles are smoothed he trades jokes with fellow musicians Miles Jackson, Craig Bignell and Mark LaLama who are also getting outfitted for the show. The small-town rural connection, where abandoned *ranges* reside in farmers' fields, is a strong connection for the community and Frank's music. In his many years on the road Frank has played in hundreds of small towns across Canada.

Children, teenagers, middle-aged and white-haired men and women bundled in heavy coats, scarves, hats, gloves and snow-covered boots pass through the high-school's exterior doors. A few men are accompanied by wives and girlfriends. The audience mulls around the theatre doors, washrooms and foyer waiting for the 8 p.m. start.

Behind the merchandise table loaded with tapes, cassettes, music books and T-shirts, John Loweth, the middle-aged, greying would-be evangelist, sporting a black blazer and dress pants, hails: "Programs, programs. Would you like a freebie? Programs will be two dollars at 8 o'clock."

"With this music book you'll sound like Frank tomorrow at 10 a.m. By 2 p.m. you can join him on stage."

"Yes, you can put that on your charge card. If you don't have one I'll lend you mine."

"Oh, a man with money. Tapes are eighteen and twenty-two dollars, CDs are twenty-five."

"Those are nice easy arrangements to play. If you practice them really good, when Frank comes to town next year, and we should need a replacement, just let us know. It might be you."

"Programs are free. But don't tell the people inside: they've just paid two dollars."

"You take the top copy. I'll keep the bottom. Frank will be coming out at the end of the performance. He'll sign that CD if you like. Take the plastic off so he can sign the inside cover. The plastic is hard to get off. Good thing you bought the CD now. You'll have two hours to figure out how to get it off."

In the theatre paper rustles, seats thunk as they flop and creak when they fill, people chatter, laugh and sneeze. At the back of the seats, Bill Girdwood, a six-foot nine, bearded sound man, with a gold earring in his left ear, checks his soundboard and utters a few muffled words into his headphone. Photographs of his children Heather, Ian, Laurie, Leah and wife Tanya rest on the top of the board. A red toy bulldog and a pink teddy bear – so-you-won't-get-lonely gifts from his daughters – face the stage. A white sheet of paper with the evening's program scribbled in thick black marker rests in the centre of the soundboard.

"Let's baste the budgie," Frank says at about one minute to eight. With heads bowed in solemn concentration, the four musicians emerge from the dressing room and begin a dash for the stage. Through scattered cables, trunks, speakers, curtains, lights and risers Miles finds his place on the keyboard, Craig perches in front of the Tupperware, aka drums, and Mark lands in front of his keyboard. Both Frank and the theatre floorman wait behind the stage curtains.

"Ready?" the theatre floorman asks Bill through his headphones.

"Yep, let's go," responds Bill. The floorman tips his head at Frank standing beside him. The lights are shut off, plunging the theatre into darkness. In smooth baritone Bill broadcasts to the eager audience: "Ladies and gentlemen, please welcome to Spruce Grove, Frank Mills." In unison, Miles, Craig and Mark play Frank's 'Rocky Mountain Sunrise.' The curtain rises and the spotlights follow Frank as he quickly seats himself at the electronic piano and joins in the familiar song. After the applause at the end of the song, Frank begins a series of jokes, anecdotes, personal history and song introductions that characterize the two-hour performance.

"They usually go off without a hitch," says Frank. "After 30 years in the business we've got the art of the road figured out, or at least we've learned enough and made enough mistakes to figure out what people want and what works." It wasn't always this smooth and polished.

An October 10, 1981 article titled 'Mills Western Tour Successful Launch for Album,' published in *RPM* magazine, records the workings of Frank's first tour in Western Canada. "Toronto: the signing of Frank Mills to Capitol, the firming of his western tour dates and the availability of his new album at retail outlets were rare happenings for a recording act, domestic or otherwise. Mills signed with Capitol on a Monday, was on the road on Wednesday and Capitol had the product in the stores by Friday.

"Bruce Davidson, who heads the Calgary-based Tanglewood Production firm that was responsible for the production, promotion and management of Mills' 12 shows in 9 days, called the tour: 'one of the most successful promotion/concert tours I have ever been associated with.' He went on to say, 'I have never had so much cooperation from a record label as I have from Capitol with the Frank Mills concert tour. They really worked their butts off in promoting Frank's new album.'

"Some of the dates weren't exactly on the mainline; so, through the assistance of Angus Aviation, an Alberta airline, three planes were made available to the Mills entourage, making for a trouble free in and out for Lethbridge, Red Deer and Ft. McMurray; other dates were Saskatoon, Edmonton, Calgary, Regina, Vancouver and Victoria. All, with the exception of Vancouver, drew packed houses.

"Mills lent himself to local radio-sponsored autograph sessions which has added much in the sales of his new album, *Prelude to Romance* from which 'Plaisir D'Amour' will be taken as a single. A check with several western retailers reveals that Mills' album is considered a long-term release with most expecting the album to be a large winner for the Christmas season. Traveling with Mills was his Calgary pick-up group, comprising ten of the city's top professional musicians. Says Davidson, 'The official Frank Mills touring band lives in Calgary.' So successful was the western tour that plans are now being laid for a major tour of eastern Canada. Davidson is expected to coordinate this tour as well."

When Frank first began touring in 1981, an orchestra, backup singers and assorted technical people trekked across the country with a grand piano and reams of sound equipment. Musical arranger and conductor Eric Freidenberg played the flute, Dave Jandrisch was on synthesizer, Ron Halderson played guitar, John Hyde played bass guitar and Garry DeBoeck performed the drums. Miles Jackson who has played keyboards with Frank since that first tour, remembers the early years: "It was big time. We were playing for 2,000 people in Toronto's Roy Thompson Hall, auditoriums, and theatres across the country. There was a full orchestra with female chick singers. Singers are singers, but when it's a chick it's a chick singer. We'd fly to all the gigs and stay in expensive hotels," recalls Miles.

In those early years putting together a two-hour show was difficult. "I didn't have much repertoire. Everybody knew my two songs, 'Music Box Dancer,' and 'Peter Piper.' But you need a lot of material for a two-hour show. We produced a film to accompany the song '401 West.' That was awful. We added chatter and stories. We tried all sorts of things. Some of it was good and some of it was bad," notes Frank.

"That first show in Lethbridge was one of the most awkward and embarrassing shows that I can recall, for me, Leonard Rambeau, Bruce Davidson and the others. Frank talked for about 15 minutes and only played for two. He wanted to chat. Not about anything in particular, he just wanted to talk. Then we said 'Frank, quit your talking and play more.' Things started to change. The show developed over the years and he fine-tuned this and that and got pretty good at it," recalls John Loweth.

"We had this entourage of people, equipment, photographers, managers. There was a lot of exciting stuff with big rooms, parties, people, food and all the trappings. Excessive, flamboyant, big time but little money. We tried a lot of things that didn't work. Frank dressed in a beanie-hat and sweater and performed 'Piano Lesson Number Five.' Lots of things got tossed because they didn't work," says Miles.

"Back then, that's what you did. The press parties, the booze. All in an attempt to get some hype to sell records. I remember one guy spending $10,000 on a party. He invited the radio and TV and newspaper people, the major buyers of all the record companies and department stores. At the party they all said, 'yeah, we'll take an order for our store.' A few weeks after the orders had been shipped out, they came back. The guy was on the hook for about $40,000. It was the era of big bucks, hype and all that stuff," remembers John. By 1986, the excesses were too much, there was little money to show for the efforts, and personalities were clashing. In an awkward position, Frank replaced Bruce Davidson. Thereafter, Paul Mascioli of Mascioli Entertainment handled the tour details until his move to Nashville. Brian Edwards took over in 1992.

"Although we had the symphony orchestra it wasn't a good show. It was difficult getting everyone coordinated and working together. The audience didn't like the show as much as they do now. Over the years the show has been trimmed so it's not overwhelming. It's smaller, just the six of us. I think Frank feels good about this. I think the show is better than ever. The musicians are better, it's manageable, it's not big time and unruly. It's a package. People like this show. You can tell because they buy his albums. They never used to do that as much," adds Miles.

While the look of the show has changed over the years, putting it together is always a logistics feat. The show that eases by in two hours takes about a year to plan. "It's like your grandmother's 80th birthday party. A year of planning is over in an hour," muses Frank. Work on a fall, spring or Christmas tour begins with Brian Edwards, Frank's booking agent, securing the venues in a certain area. That can mean 14 gigs in 16 days, or 26 gigs in 28 days in theatres, halls, churches, auditoriums, cultural centres, colleges, opera houses, community centres and schools. "We coordinate the dates, handle the advertising and act as an agent for anyone who wants to book Frank. At times, it's like throwing darts at a road map because you never know what areas will be good and what areas will be bad. One area that did well last year, may be a bust this year. That's the business. You don't know what the crowds and ticket sales will be like," says Brian Edwards.

After Brian secures the venues, Bill Girdwood, the soundman and technical director, handles the tour details. He estimates driving times between destinations, contacts the venue's technical director to determine risers, lighting, spots and sound for that performance, rents sound equipment and secures a truck to haul the appendages. After he's gathered all those details, he develops a tour schedule which includes dates, cities, venues, hotels, phone numbers, contact names and travel information. As the official hotel booker, Bill has mastered the art of avoiding sleepless nights, the hard way:

* Spend the extra ten bucks on a good hotel. We're not talking the Hilton, just a reasonable chain hotel. At a cheap hotel on the edge of town, you'll wake up with a bad back from sleeping on a lumpy mattress. Your nose will be stuffed from inhaling smoke and you'll probably be kept awake by the jackhammers or trains pounding all night. You might be awakened during the night by a street urchin singing Merry Christmas. Frank is grumpy when he hasn't had enough sleep.

* If there is construction or remodeling going on, ask to be placed as far as possible from the activity, so you won't choke on paint fumes or risk an

ugly confrontation involving a rudely-awakened, half-clothed musician screaming Beatles lyrics at an early-rising church group.

* Always carry survival gear: ear plugs, extra batteries, Tylenol, books, credit cards, magazines, beer.

* Try to avoid staying at friends' houses. While they mean well, they might forget to tell you that the cat sleeps with you, the plumbers are coming at seven and it's a transition time in their marriage (with the permission of their therapist they'll verbalize their feelings at any time).

* Remember the name of the hotel you booked before. If you forget, you'll have to keep Frank busy until the evening. If Frank sees the sleazy hotel at night, it won't be so bad. Maybe he won't realize you booked the wrong hotel.

About three weeks to a month prior to the gig, Brian coordinates media interviews. He'll send out press releases and media kits to local television, radio, magazine and newspaper editors in the area. Hopefully, some media people interview Frank and print or broadcast the upcoming concert. From Vermont or Nassau, Frank slots two to three consecutive days to conduct marathon question and answer sessions.

Frank recalls good and bad interviews. Early morning television interviews were difficult: "If I don't get eight hours sleep, I'm shot. I can't think. I can't speak. I'm just no good at them. I hate doing these. The worst part is that you arrive at a television station and wait several hours before they interview you. In television it is "hurry up and wait."

At times it's frustrating to have media people ask him the same questions all the time. Frank's best interview was with Peter Gzowski on CBC. Interviews with Carl Banas in Toronto and Paul Reid in Montreal are among the most memorable. "There were many critics who came to my concerts having no business being there. Because 'Music Box Dancer' had risen to number one, most newspapers sent their rock 'n' roll reporter (complete with bare chest, gold chain and hip lingo) to interview a guy who would rather have talked to *Country Journal*. In bewilderment, they didn't have the musical knowledge to understand my music. Dennis Hunt of the paper *Record World* in LA was the worst.

"One time, a critic compared the performance to a crease in my pants. That bothered me. I didn't care if they criticized my music, that was their job. But it was very hurtful when they attacked me personally."

Meanwhile, John determines how many cassettes, CDs, music books, T-shirts, and programs he'll need for the first few days of the tour. More items will be couriered to the site during the tour. "Basting the budgie" kicks off from a designated location. (In roadie lingo, each show is a "budgie," each one must be basted. That is, making a small thing out of a show which by now you've probably done 20 times in the last 20 days). Frank (aka the Captain, Uncle Frank), John (aka the Loweth Form of the Law, Lobby Gandhi, the Loweth Form of Life, Johnny Swag), Craig (aka Craigorich, Cake) and Mark (pronounced like a dog barking with a hairlip) travel in a rented passenger van. Bill (aka Willie, Bilge (because he's always burping)) and Miles (aka Milsey, Knit Face) ride in the equipment van. Collectively, the six band members are known as the "bitches." Bill and Miles usually leave around 9 a.m. to ensure an arrival time about 3-4 hours before the show. After checking into the hotel, Bill takes Miles to the library. Depending on the outcome, Miles stays there or goes back to the hotel. Sometimes the library won't let Miles check his e-mail because he's not a local resident.

Bill heads back to the venue to set up the equipment, about a three-hour job. For every gig Bill plugs and connects and assembles speakers, cords, microphones, soundboard, keyboards, risers, monitors, drums, music stands, headphones and fastens down wires with duct tape. "We all take the job seriously. Making Frank sound as good as possible is our goal. We are a group of guys out there having fun, and I think the audience responds to that," says Bill Girdwood.

He assembles the electronic piano – an electronic keyboard resting on a plywood Steinway piano – in about 10 minutes. The piano was modeled after a nine-foot concert Steinway, and scaled down to a more portable seven foot six model. In previous years, a "real" piano accompanied the tour. Other times, Bill had to find one from a local school, music company or the venue. Most times, a dust-ridden, moth-eaten out-of-tune contraption was resurrected from a storage room or closet. Over the years, the group has spent thousands of dollars locating pianos, moving them, tuning them and moving them back. Several years ago Bill had an electronic piano made that is stored in a black box, comes apart easily, assembles readily and bears a remarkable resemblance to the real thing. Even better, Frank says it's always in tune and he gets to play on the same piano every night. Between concerts, the electronic piano resides in the back of thc shop at Mayfair Music, John's publishing company in Markham, Ontario.

Sometime between noon and 2 p.m., Frank, John, Craig and Mark check into the hotel, view the evening's venue, tour the local mall, have lunch, go back to the hotel and wait. With idle time, Miles, Craig and Mark might compose songs such as 'Christmas in the Lobby.'

'Christmas in the Lobby'
(sung to the tune of 'Christmas in the Trenches')
by Miles Jackson, Craig Bignell, Mark LaLama

My name is Johnny Loweth and I'm from Ontario
I sell the CDs, books and tapes at every Frank Mills show.
The merchandise is neatly stacked, and when the folks arrive,
I put my sales pitch into overdrive...

I know the blue hairs have the cash. I've seen it all before.
But 15 minutes isn't long to empty out the store.
Me Mom is first to cross the floor, her fifty held up high.
And soon the rest come up behind to buy...

"Don't play that tape when you're alone," says I to one old gal.
"You'll get so excited by yourself, you'll wish you had a pal!"
"You'll play like Frank tomorrow if you buy this book today!"
But from the back, I heard a small voice say...

'Tis Christmas in our small town, and you're taking all our cash,
My husband is still unemployed, our car is out of gas,
The children don't have much to eat, the dog just passed away,
There'll be no gifts for us on Christmas day."

'How 'bout a tape?" says I to her, "I'll make you a such a deal.
Your tale of woe has touched me in a place I seldom feel...
I'll charge you only twenty bucks and eat the GST."
I heard her softly mutter, "I'll take three..."

'Twas Christmas in the lobby, the tapes were moving well.
Some said the CDs were too high, but I said, "No, they'll sell"
I jacked the prices up a buck and moved them to the front.
It's just another Loweth selling stunt.

(Key change up)

Some say it's rude to grab the cash without a hint of shame.
But every time the crowds press near, I do it just the same.
Some say I'm stooping pretty low, "How can you sleep at night?"
That's why I'm called the "Loweth form of life."

'Twas Christmas in the lobby, the tapes were moving well.
Some said the CDs were too high, but I said, "No, they'll sell"
I jacked the prices up a buck and moved them to the front.
It's just another Loweth selling stunt.

After lunch, Frank takes a nap. Then he might be interviewed by a media person. After that, he reads a book in his hotel room and waits until sound check, between six and seven p.m. at the venue. Even after years of practice, minor glitches happen. Something gets unplugged, something falls apart, a plug has a loose wire, plugs get switched or something gets attached into the wrong thing. After the half-hour sound check to make sure everything works, it's back to the dressing rooms to dress, exchange jokes, news and other trivia as the audience arrives. Frank may do another media interview before the show. By 7:45 p.m., it's usually a full house.

After the show, it takes Bill about an hour to take apart the piano, bundle the equipment and stack the truck. Meanwhile, Frank is signing autographs, record albums, T-shirts and programs in the foyer. Around 10:30 p.m. the show's excitement quickly fades as the venue manager locks the front door, leaving behind a quiet, somber place.

After John has gathered the unsold items, the "bitches" head to the local pub or back to the hotel room for a "little swill." English pubs, where stuffed moose, bear, grouse, partridge, owl and hawk adorn the walls, weathered floorboards creak, railroad rafters support the ceiling and the smell of smoke and beer linger among the patrons, are favorite spots for unwinding after the concert. Over beer and wine the "bitches" joke about the budgie basting, clams (mistakes the audience didn't pick up), train wrecks (when each guy simultaneously lost his place), hitting the rhubarb (losing your place while playing (like driving off the road, into the ditch and into the rhubarb)), John's fast-slow-fast-slow-fast-slow driving habits, Craig's latest harvest, the newest addition to Mark's accordion collection, John's new lines at the merchandise table, Bill's latest haircut and various road tales. The "boys" frequently tease Frank about playing too fast during the performance (Hayward Parrott has been saying that about Frank for years). Mark adds stories about his life on the road with Ken Munshaw, Liberty Silver, George Fox, Susan Aglukart and Amy Sky. Craig and Bill interject with their own accounts of people and tours with George Fox and Susan Aglukart. There are no beer-bottles-flying, motorcycles-in-the-hallway or loud, all-out parties typical of some punk rock and heavy metal bands. At the hotel they watch TV, order in pizza, play cards and tell stories. They'll leave the pub when the lights are turned out. At a Tim Hortons or Harvey's they'll discuss philosophy and the meaning of life. The day ends at 1 a.m. or 3 a.m., when one tipsy, blurry-eyed band member says, "Maybe it's time for bed, huh?"

They'll begin again at 9:00 or 10:00 a.m. the next morning. Everybody sleeps or chills all day and then comes alive at night. Over the years, the motley crew have traveled Canada from coast to coast. In the east, the Atlantic waves crash against sheer rocky headlands where old canneries and wood-frame buildings have been restored, commercial fishing boats line the docks, nets are hung out to dry and fishermen sell lobster right off the boats. In the west, the rumbling Pacific surf pounds hard-packed, sandy beaches lined by dense rain forest. In the north, silent icebergs are larger than battleships, rolling, treeless tundra stretches out to the horizon, and there are numerous emerald lakes and craggy snow-clad peaks. In the prairies, fields of golden wheat ripple in the wind, arrow-straight highways and flat tableland stretch out to the horizon, punctuated only by little clusters of villages and grain elevators. They've also ventured to locations in the US and on international soil.

Frank likens the art of the road to the rocumentary *Spinal Tap*. This video is a hilarious comedy about a fictitious heavy metal band that once upon a time had a pretty big hit song. Now, nearly two decades later, members of *Spinal Tap* still cling to some glint of their lost glory as they embark on an accident-plagued tour across America. In Cleveland, the group gets lost underneath the stage. In Washington, they're accidentally booked at an Air Force formal dance. And in a Chicago record store, no one shows up to get their autographs.

Frank and the boys have experienced their own *Spinal Tap*. With time to spare before a concert, Frank and John visited Magnetic Hill outside Moncton, New Brunswick. They parked the van and straddled the barricades blocking the closed tourist site. At the province's best-known oddity, cars driven downhill to a certain point seem to coast back uphill when the engine is turned off and the brakes released. After the *wosh* of a gale nearly knocked the two roadies over, John asked Frank, "Do you still have your clothes on?" "I'm not sure," responded the puzzled Frank.

On one tour everyone except Frank shaved his head. Frank dubbed that tour 'Frankie and the Skinheads.' John earned the new nickname 'Lobby Gandhi' for his resemblance to the hero. "When you're out on the road for a month or more you don't see people you know. You sometimes do weird things," says Craig Bignell.

On another tour, an inebriated mayor – who thought Eric was Frank – presented Eric with keys to the city. On another occasion, a mayor gave Frank a huge framed reproduction of the city. Frank lugged the print around to keep it in reasonable shape. Thinking Frank didn't want it, and not sure how he would get it on the plane to Nassau, John gave it away to a local promoter who was at the show. Just as the promoter was leaving that night, Frank retrieved the painting. Later in the tour, the picture disappeared.

During a performance on a Christmas tour, a nervous choir member threw up all over the stage. Another time Craig missed his cue at the end of the evening performance and Frank kept bowing and bowing and bowing and bowing.

On one winter tour, Miles, the nervous back seat driver, didn't think John could drive through snow and took to the wheel. Driving between Rosetown and Saskatoon, Miles applied the breaks on a red light sending the van and its frightened passengers into oncoming traffic and near death. Miles hasn't driven since.

Each tour gets branded with the name of some funny event or person. Throughout the tour, the event or person is the object of fun and ridicule. Leftover lobsters dubbed a maritime tour. Wanting to treat the band, Frank ordered lobsters for an after show dinner. Eric was allergic to the critters, two guys were vegetarians, and John doesn't like lobster. Frank and Miles bought a cooler from the local hardware store and ice from the 7-Eleven. They trucked the leftover critters throughout the remainder of the tour. On the "lobster tour" Frank and Miles sat on the picnic tables at Wendy's or Harvey's eating lobster tails and drinking beer while the rest of the band ate hamburgers.

There was a "cappuccino tour" and in 1998, the "garlic tour" named in honor of Craig's home grown pungent bulb. In 1998, the spring tour was in southern Ontario. Craig returned to his farm each night, within driving distance of the venue, and returned the next morning with a fresh supply of garlic cloves. Before the show and during the intermission, the wreaking "bitches" feasted on crackers, garlic spread with Tabasco sauce, bagels and cheese spread.

Another year, a policeman who spoke with a lateral lisp drew the rib. That policeman pulled over the van intending to give the driver a ticket. When he realized Frank was in the van he said, "I can't give you a ticket, I'm going to your concert tonight." At the concert that evening, on the "lateral lisp" tour, Frank gave the officer a bouquet of flowers.

Another tour was dubbed in honor of Chuckie's wife. While in St. John's, Newfoundland, the band stopped into Chuckie's Fish and Chips, an "authentic" fish and chips establishment. An oriental lady (wife of the owner Chuckie) asked the boys if they would like some "flinch flies." "We were expecting an authentic Newfoundlander," laughs Miles.

The last night of the tour – when the budgie is finally basted – is joke night. Bill concocts funny and harmless practical jokes. "We (the band) are usually victims of Bill's joke playing. These "stunts" may occur before or during a performance," says Mark LaLama. Bill spreads garlic cloves on the floor, speakers and music stands, tells hysterical jokes into the guys' headphones during the show (Craig, Miles and Mark have headphones, sans Frank), displays beer bottles on top of the piano, places chicken in the rafters (during the show it lands on the keyboards or in someone's lap), attaches sticky notes to music sheets, puts obscene things under stools, plays Santana music or comedy tapes into headphones, pours water on the seats or fills the stage with plungers. "During one Christmas tour Bill put some unflattering pictures between the music sheets. When I was turning the pages the wind caught them. I tried to grab some of the pictures on the way down. One of the photos landed picture-side-up in front of the choir," remembers Craig.

Depending upon departure times and travel connections, there may or may not be a debriefing session at the hotel or a local pub. Frequently, band members fly or drive home directly after the final performance. The last few days of the tour are always the toughest and longest as the "bitches" come closer to being home rather than a hotel room across the country.

For the "bitches" life is an assortment of arteries, turnpikes, freeways, six-lane highways, four-lane or two-lane highways and thoroughfares. The road depicts the struggles of the musicians' soul; the struggle for fame and fortune against home and family; the demands and temptations of the road that are loved and hated almost equally. The weird sleep-play-drive-sleep ritual contradicts the wild and crazy lore one hears about life on the road. It's not glamorous. At times it's boring, mundane, routine and hard. The road seems endless with look-alike, taste-alike Tim Hortons, Pizza-Huts, Burger-Kings, venues, hotels and crowds.

On the road, Mark – who is away at least one week per month (sometimes more) – talks to his pre-school daughters, three-year-old Breton, and one-year-old Dominique, every day. Breton and Dominique fax dad pictures while Mark sends them postcards. "When I'm on the road a lot, I miss my family too much," comments Mark.

Some years, Craig says he's barely finished one tour when he's on the plane for the next one. He's away so much of the time that his dog bites him because he doesn't recognize him. "Some times you don't lie down for three days. One time I had to catch a red eye flight to Toronto. I arrived at 6:00 a.m., just in time to catch the 6:30 a.m. flight to another gig," notes Craig. Half-way on a 24-day tour, you're sick at the thought of your wife having to stay up all night with your daughter. Or you're in Switzerland when your daughter is born ("We tried to plan for it, but she came early," says Bill). You make sure your kid's birthday present is bought before you go. Or, you'll have to get your wife to buy it and sign your name.

Life is especially hard when family difficulties have to be managed from 3,000 miles away. One year, Bill experienced difficulties with his ex-wife and "school problems" with his children. In the midst of moving to a new home, Jacqueline, Mark's wife had snarls with a neighbor. The lady was arrested after repeated threats to Jacqueline's safety. On another tour, Craig was concerned about getting a mortgage for the new farm. "It's hard to be miles away when there are problems at home," notes Craig.

The art of the road is also about trying to eat nutritious food. It's trying not to add extra pounds when you're eating in restaurants, fullfat cafes and pizza joints. You've already had breakfast but you'd like a side order of eggs because you're still hungry. The restaurant doesn't serve side orders of eggs. To get the eggs you have to order stacka' cakes (pancakes) and eggs. You end up eating the eggs and the stacka' cakes and kicking yourself all the way to the next gig. It's waking up at 1:00 a.m. to the smell of pizza that Bill's just ordered. You can't get back to sleep so you stay up until 4:00 a.m. drinking beer and eating dough and pepperoni and cheese and tomatoes. It's an unending search for food that's not too badly fried, overcooked, salted or bland. It's too much coffee and doughnuts at Tim Hortons, little exercise, too many drinks, snacks, and dinner late at night.

"Ernie," aka electric pot, helps Mark and Craig prepare healthy food. The granola-health-food duo cooks pasta, rice, couscous and other delights. The brew is seasoned with lots of garlic and hot peppers. "There is a wonderful smell in the hotel room. It smells awesome," laughs Craig.

On the long drives there's little to do except watch the prairie, sea, rolling hills or mountain landscape drift by. Everytime Bill and Miles pass an auto wrecker's Bill repeats the comment made by a member of George Fox's band: it's either an auto wrecker's or a blue grass festival. The road takes you away from your wife and kids. The only time you have at home is spent with the family. So the band becomes your only social contact. The cities and towns look like one long suburban sprawl. The road drives you crazy with insomnia. You wonder if you'll make it home in time for Christmas (one year in Edmonton, it was so cold that the pilot couldn't start the plane. When the airline rerouted Frank through Chicago, Miami and Nassau, rather than the usual Toronto, Miami and Nassau, he arrived home earlier than normal). The hotel bed is too soft or too hard. Sometimes you wake up with a raw throat because there were no non-smoking rooms left. The road leads you to new demands and into new temptations. Time on the road is elongated, at times, meaningless. There are the groupies who wait until the last light bulb dims, to catch a glimpse and shake hands with "the star."

On the other hand, many performers like the road. It's a time warp with no family responsibilities, no snow to shovel, no walls to re-paint, and no crying babies to remind them of another life off the stage. There are career highlights as when Frank played with symphony orchestras across the country. To John, the road is a welcome change from his routine, daily office work. For Bill, it's an opportunity to connect with friends. "I don't have friends at home anymore. When I'm home I spend the time with my family. Being on the road is 'going out with the boys.' "

Craig agrees. "It's like a family. We haven't seen each other for so long but when we get back together it's like it never ended. It's more than playing music. Yes, we play and do our work. But so many times there are personal things going on during the tour. We are there for each other during these difficult times." Craig say the road is also about the rural connection between friends. "There's Frank with his homes, John lives in the country, I live on a farm in an Amish community, Mark just bought a farm, Miles lives at Ma-Me-O Beach and Bill lives in Halifax. We're not so "music" focused. We talk about other things. I've worked with many musicians who only talk about music and their hits. Nothing else matters to them but making it to the top. They don't care about their marriage or their kids. I remember one tour Frank was considering buying a new trailer for his tractor. He brought along the pictures. He couldn't decide between the four-wheeled model or the two-wheeled model. It's not all music on the tours. We all have personal lives that carry on regardless of the tours. We've been through some good tours and some bad tours. We've also been through a great deal of personal stuff. None of us has an "attitude." We're not "stars" out there, we're real people with wives and families. There's Frank who makes maple syrup and goes fishing. He has a personality. He is real."

A musician's life is a constant struggle between the nurturing, sensitive person society says he ought to be and the driven artist who must embrace selfishness if creativity is to survive. He works on that never ending office called "the road." Frank looks forward to the day when he won't have to go there: "I'm looking forward to having a normal life. You get tired of being on the road. You long for home. You want to have a quiet, relaxed "normal" life. There are other songs to write, more maples to tap and other places to cruise to with Sir Geoffrey."

8

LIFE MUSIC

"Feel the flush of romantic passion.
Fantasize about running away with the man or woman of your dreams.
Mess up.
Blow up.
Put aside treasured dreams.
Drown in a quagmire of pain and confusion.
Grope with a betrayal.
Rejoice in the beauty of a crimson sunset.
Run. Fall down. Get up. Start all over.
Taste the sweet innocence of first love.
Flunk a chemistry exam.
Weep when your mother is laid to rest.
Question the road you travel.
Let love blind you to reality.
Darn socks.

Wonder what an old girlfriend or boyfriend is doing on Friday night.

Ask a friend to pray for you when you don't know what else to do.

Feel like you're going nowhere.

Risk a new relationship. Be hurt. Avoid anything resembling love for the rest of your life.

Reflect on a life that is now three-fourths over.

Ponder the boredom of housework.

Wonder if the man or woman you left behind will still want you.

Get stuck in traffic.

Ban the savage fantasies that snare you.

Remember that bloody, seething argument with your spouse.

Be in love with the ocean.

Be outraged about the contents of the 6 o'clock news.

Envy another's love relationship.

On your knees, feel the old tears and grief and shake off the invisible assailants.

Rationalize over cheating on a lover.

Spear fish for grouper in the Caribbean.

Contemplate how different you are (or how much alike you are) from your mother, brother, sister or friend.

Agonize over never seeing a lover again.

Live with failure and still stand on the edge of a lake and shout to the silver of the full moon, "Yes."

Be opened by life's betrayals. Become shriveled and closed for fear of further pain.

Weep over shattered dreams.

Issue a deep belly laugh about yourself.

Think about the love/hate aspects of an intense relationship.

Decide you're not going to take it anymore.

Fly kites.

Explore the sad choices of a pregnant teenager.

Listen to conversations in the grocery store checkout.

Lose your belief in humanity.

Remember when you got fired from a job.

See beauty even when it is not pretty everyday.

Imagine what life might be like if you had made another choice.

Remember how your father or mother or sister or brother or friend or lover disappointed you.

Be horrified at the daily newspaper's account of devastating floods in Taiwan.

Get mad at the same commercial repeated throughout the movie.

Tell yourself you can enjoy ice cream anytime you want.

Ache for something.

Risk looking like a fool for love, for your dream, for the adventure of being alive.

Touch the centre of your own sorrow.

Spend three days climbing to the top of a mountain. Scream when you get there.

And then write songs," says Frank. Songwriting is an art in which people create songs by mixing together words and music, not unlike an alchemist mixing disparate elements to make gold. The substance of those songs are the pains, joys, sorrows, griefs, questions, triumphs, failures and victories of our own experience in this journey we call life. Songwriting is the music of that life – life music. To do both well – write songs and live fully – Frank suggests we ought to live intensely, enjoying and savoring the experience of life in its many forms.

The sea, salt and moisture have been unkind to Frank's music awards and his piano. He gave his Heinzman grand piano (the one he had shipped from Toronto when he moved to the island) to a church in Nassau. Many of his tattered, rusted and worn music awards are retired to the closet. The 1981 William Harold Moon Award and SOCAN Classic Awards for 'Music Box Dancer,' and 'Love Me, Love Me, Love,' however, hold the highest place of honor in his studio. "These awards are the most important to me because that's me, the writer. They're the first thing you see when you walk into my studio," says Frank.

He speaks from personal experience, frustration and success on living and writing intensely. Frank is most frequently asked the question "How do you write a song?" He says songwriting is like writing a letter. "It's an art, like anything else. You receive a letter from someone and you respond to it. You receive input and inspiration. The idea is the letter you receive, which prompts a response. For a song, the emotion prompts a response. The songwriter responds by expressing himself."

Even the greatest and most enduring songs begin where all songs start – with a single idea or spark of inspiration gleaned from some life experience. "Life experiences give you the fodder for songs. But you have to pay attention to those happenings. The more you allow life to unfold before you, the more you can reach into that creative capacity. Then you'll be able to write songs." The gift of songwriting is the gift of knowing and communicating – the words and music that name the thoughts inside people's minds, the words that mask the fears and secrets inside their hearts. According to Frank, to do this, one must see, hear, listen, feel and experience, intensely. Perhaps that's why there is an illusion, a sense of mystery about those individuals who consider themselves songwriters. While they are human beings who dwell in the ordinary realm, they create what seems to be so extraordinary.

What is a successful song?

To be successful, to be meaningful and memorable, a song must be complete in itself. What makes a John Lennon, Jimmy Webb or Duke Ellington? Universally, successful songs are well-crafted musically and lyrically. As for commercial success, that is another matter entirely. Songs defy classification. It's difficult to predict what song – whether country and western, rock, pop, blues, jazz – might bring commercial success. Writing songs is art and as much luck as it is craft, determination and persistence. Generally speaking, David Baskerville, Ph.D., writing in *Music Business Handbook and Career Guide*, says great songs tend to exhibit six characteristics:

"1. The song is memorable. It sticks in the mind, primarily through the use of a hook – a catchy phrase or refrain that repeats several times during the song.

2. The song has instant appeal.

3. The song relies on imagery so listeners can "see" something.

4. The song has a beginning, middle and an end.

5. There is a central theme to the song.

6. A song has an element of mystery, an indefinable enchantment that transports the listener.

Going a step further to attain commercial success, Baskerville says four additional steps are needed:

1. The song gets an appealing initial performance, particularly by a well-known performer.

2. The recording company promotes strong airplay for the recording.

3. The song and the recording suit the taste of the current market.

4. The recording is effectively distributed and is made readily available nationally."

After a lifetime in the business, Frank is surprized at his own success with his little tinkly piano piece – 'Music Dance Box Dancer' – what Michael Hoppe called, 'Music Box Whatever.' "The only thing I've been able to figure is that it is a happy song. It is a piano piece that anybody can play. It's everybody's dream of being a piano player. When the song hit the charts, all the piano players of the world came out. Here was this song on the radio you heard every ten minutes, and you could play it. We have three versions, a basic piece, an intermediate level and the advanced version. I think that appeals to a lot of wanna-be piano players. Here is this piece by an international artist, and I can play it at home," says Frank.

John Loweth adds his comments about the unplanned success. "When it first came out, we received letters from piano teachers wanting it for their students. People wanted to use it at weddings, grandmother's birthday, whatever. Everyone fancied that song. Timing was a factor. We were in the middle of the disco era. People were looking for something different. Everything was right for an instrumental hit."

The craft

Frank believes that songwriting is for the determined. Songwriting is a serious craft, like sculpting, carpentry, engineering or medicine. While songwriting relies on inspiration, songwriters must balance the inspiration that seems to come from somewhere beyond with the craft that comes from years of work. The craft is at the service of inspiration. This gives confidence and a dependable vehicle to communicate the inspirations in an enjoyable and easily understood format. "Many people send me songs. Most of the songs are written from a single event, a failed love, the death of a child or a happy incident. People write a song about the misfortune, thinking it will be a great song. Yes, it's tragic that these events happen. Yes, people write these songs honestly. It may have worked once or twice that these songs did become a hit, but it rarely does. Songwriting is more than that. Songwriting is the sum of all your life experiences. If you are songwriter, you incorporate everything that has happened to you into your writing. You don't just sit down one day and write one song. You write all the time because that's who you are," adds Frank.

He continues, "Most people don't realize that songwriting is a craft and an art. The more you do it the better you get at it. Most of the songwriters I know are like any other writer. They have a project to complete, work to do, a living to make. It's hardly ever simply inspiration. While something may inspire you to write a song, that inspiration comes from devoting yourself to the craft of songwriting, not just writing "a song." After many years of writing songs you learn how to take those bits of inspiration and craft them into something. It takes a long time to know how to connect words, music and life experience."

Frank says he is puzzled at the definition of a songwriter. For tax purposes, SOCAN defines a songwriter as someone who writes two songs a year. "That's not a songwriter. That's someone who's never going to get anywhere. You've got to write 50, 100, 200, 500 songs. Then throw them away. Maybe one, five or even 10 will survive as a good song. This is how it's done. Songwriting is work and it's not marvelous. But there is a deep sense of satisfaction, after going through that process in arriving at some soul stirring work. Songwriting is an activity of the soul. It is a means of becoming closer to the mundane aspects of everyday living. And then you have to communicate that mundanity to the rest of the world. That's what songwriting is, telling the world about life, much of which is boring and ordinary and the same."

Frank frequently refers to Canadian writer and singer Gordon Lightfoot's hit single, 'The Wreck of the Edmund Fitzgerald' as his favorite example of the power of inspiration combined with craft. Lightfoot got the idea for the song by reading an article in *Newsweek* detailing the shipwreck on Lake Superior of the iron ore carrier 'Edmund Fitzgerald,' which sank in a gale with all 29 men on board in November 1975. "He took the facts and addressed the emotions behind them. Everybody knew the boat sank. The headline said '29 Men Die in Shipwreck.' That's normal, mundane, everyday. Gordon turned it into something stirring; the church bell chimed till it rang 29 times for each man on the 'Edmund Fitzgerald.' This is writing. You don't do this once in a lifetime. You do it because you are a songwriter.

"It was an awful storm. But again, Gordon presented the emotion and feelings behind the headlines: Does anybody know where the love of God goes when the waves turn the minutes to hours? That's songwriting." Lightfoot, who sailed his own vessel on Lake Superior, knew the mystique of water travel and the vicious winds. The song is akin to listening to a national anthem. The musical dirge and the lyric intensity of the story-telling compels all listeners to pause and listen to the sweet elegy of 29 lives lost in the frigid waters of Lake Superior.

"I'm not saying that inspiration doesn't happen. Sometimes you wake up inspired because you dreamed about something. But songwriters are craftsman like anybody else. They put together from the unknown an expression that usually involves an expression about the known. You extract that. You create it. You pull it up from the depths and corners of your soul."

'Tears in Heaven' is another of Frank's favorite examples. Eric Clapton wrote the tribute following the death of his four-year-old-son Conor in March 1991. "If that had been written by an amateur, "the song" would have been about the grief over the loss of a child. With Clapton, certainly there was a measure of grief, but because he is a songwriter, he crafted that whole experience into an event. If you listen to the song, it's like you're walking the road with him. He has re-created the tragedy in a song. While both songs were inspired by the same event, both destroyed by sadness and grief, the amateur could have only done it once in a lifetime. Clapton does it all the time because that's what he is."

Listen and learn

Frank advises, "To write songs, listen to them. Every kind of music you can imagine. Challenge yourself." While listening, Frank recommends taking note of what you like, what sends goosebumps down your back, what moves you, what stirs you and evokes a physical or emotional reaction. For a while, many people copy this music. In time, they invent their own version.

Like food, music has different effects on different people. Some people like hot and spicy chili while others like mild spinach salad. Each food affects people temperamentally and physically. We may crave the rich and sensual foods of strawberry shortcake, hot fudge sundae, lobster or steak. Yet, a simple meal of rice, vegetables and chicken may be more nutritionally beneficial. It is the same with music. While we are fed well with a variety of music, certain forms of music may bring order, stability and inspiration to our creative efforts. Music is frequently a creative mood trigger. The word music comes from the Greek Muses, the legendary goddesses of the arts and sciences. As music is processed on both sides of the brain, listening to it primes the mind to be both artist and scientist, intuitive and logical. Music can coordinate right-brain imagery with left-brain analysis to help solve problems more creatively, generate imagery to remove creative blocks and expand perceptual horizons. Listen to anything you can, including:

Classical music. No musical style offers a greater range of tempo, dynamics, meter, pitch, texture and timbre than classical. This category includes Baroque (Handel, Vivaldi, Corelli), romantic (Schubert, Tchaikovsky, Chopin and Liszt) and impressionist music (Debussy, Ravel). "There's more music in one Bach fugue than in all the history of rock 'n' roll," insists Frank. In Debussy's 'Prelude to the Afternoon of the Faun,' the falling flute resembles a cool compress while the harp adds a soothing strum. The thrilling 'Amen' finish of Haydn's final movement from 'The Creation' resounds with the celebration of new life. A virtuoso soloist spins spine-tingling violin lines in Korngold's 'Violin Concerto, 1st movement.'

South American music. The lively beat of the Salsa, Rhumba, and Macarena can set the heart racing and get the entire body moving.

African music. Jazz, Blues, Dixieland, Soul, Calypso and Reggae that come from the expressive African heritage, convey wit and irony, affirm our humanity, inspire, uplift and release deep joy and sadness.

Big band, pop, top 40, country and western. These forms of music cover every decade imaginable from early country twang to its current status.

Rock music. Nothing beats Elvis Presley, the Rolling Stones or Michael Jackson to stir the passions, stimulate movement, release tension and mask pain. Some people, however, find this music loud, unpleasant and disturbing.

Gregorian Chant and *New Age music* can induce a state of relaxation for quiet study and meditation.

Sacred, gospel and *religious music* can provide a broader, grander view and lead to feelings of deep peace and spiritual awareness.

The music basics

To write songs one must know the language of music. An understanding of music can help the songwriter analyze such devices as form, melody, chord structure, rhythm patterns and create better lyrics that fit the color of the music. "I regret not applying myself when I was at McGill. At the time, I had to get the business thing out of my system. I regret my academic record and not working. I could have worked harder, learned more and taken it more seriously. Back then, I didn't care. I was wounded. It was very complicated. Who knows? If I had stayed on to complete a degree or diploma, I might have done better in music." Interestingly, neither Galt McDermott (composer of Hair) nor Burt Bacharach (composer of many US hits) completed degrees in music at McGill University.

Richard Lawton, dean, faculty of music, McGill University reports that a good musical education should include the following: a principal instrument (voice or instrument); performing experience (musicianship, keyboard proficiency, sight singing, dictation); theory (reading and writing skills, analysis, history); music technology (recording, programming).

With this background a songwriter can understand the musical syntax on a wider social and cultural fabric, investigate ways music can communicate meaning as well as how and why musical styles change, develop sound critical thinking, and understand how specific pieces of music are put together. From this a songwriter can understand the basic qualities of a song:

INTRODUCTION: Introductions on top 40 hits set the stage for the main melody. These short introductions, not longer than 10-15 seconds, allow a radio DJ to plug the song before it is played.

SIMPLE MELODY: This is the memorable part of the song, the collection of notes and theme that stick in the mind. A simple melody like 'Music Box Dancer,' should be based on a short theme, be easy to sing, play and remember and be repeated often so that the song is easily recognized and identified. The melody is a catchy tune you just can't get out of your head, instantly recognize and sing along to. When a really good melody emerges, one that digs deep and just won't let go, people sing it in the shower, car, while working or washing dishes. We celebrate the magic of a great melody by listening to it over and over.

CONTRASTING THEMES: The form of the song is based on the repetition of the main melody, or blocks of melody. Between each block of main melody, contrasting, short themes are injected, called a bridge. Bridges like together blocks of melody. Bridges are also used to create a particular intensity or feeling, setting the stage for the next block of melody. A bridge, or contrasting theme, always compliments and supports the main melody.

DEFINITE BEAT: Rhythmic patterns are repeated to create the feel and mood of the song.

LYRICS: Lyric patterns follow and support the main melody. When writing music, what usually begins as a mood develops into a mental picture (a dusty old barn, a crowded bar). In simple words and expressions the lyrics may tell a story, state a fact, describe a feeling or ask a question. Lyrics should present the idea in a progressive, cohesive manner.

TITLE: To remember it, the title should be composed of the fewest possible words. It should catch attention and arouse interest, be relative to contemporary life and be repeated often in the lyrics.

ORIGINALITY: The song should take the mundane, everyday, normal, and turn it into something interesting. Trade the facts for fantasy. Instead of saying the 'waves hit the beach,' create the picture 'the ebb tide lands a kiss on the shore."

HOOK: This is something in the song that immediately catches the listener's attention. A hook might be the main melody, a few notes, a chord sequence or a sound effect that appear several times in the song.

Commercial songs follow no strict format regarding the order of appearance of its introduction, chorus, verses, bridge. Most songs start with a brief, four-bar music introduction with its own, distinct melody. The introduction leads to the first and second verse, to the chorus, bridge, back to the verses, chorus, bridge, chorus, end. In a popular or commercial song, two distinct parts formed of verses and a chorus are repeated at intervals. The refrain, or chorus, establishes the main melodic and lyric theme which is different from the verses. The verses expand and explain the lyric idea set up in the chorus.

A successful songwriter arranges these tones and forms patterns, which, when combined, result in simple melodies that musically relate to each other and have a harmonious flow pleasing to the ear.

Developing a "life consciousness"

Songwriting is an act of collusion, proposes Frank. The songwriter and the listener engage in a conspiracy, and through the imperfect system of sound and lyrics, the two cooperate to make a world. We accompany Johnny Cash through the prison gates as he wails the 'Folsom Prison Blues.' We cry over never having the recipe to "bake another cake," (run out of time) in Jimmy Webb's 'MacArthur Park.' A hotel, in 'Hotel California' really talks about the drug culture, "You can check in anytime you like but you can never leave."

A songwriter can develop an antenna for turning everyday situations into potential song ideas. Life is full of drama. Ordinary, everyday events are good sources for songs. The unusual sayings and phrases, the daily occurrences can be translated into something that stirs an emotion and paints a picture. Life – and our observation and participation in it – is the ultimate creative consultant. Without the inspiration that comes from experiencing life, all the tools and gizmos in the world won't help you write a song.

"Where do songs come from?" is another question Frank has frequently been asked. "They come from anywhere, everywhere, anybody, anything and everybody," he says. The ideas come from reading a book, viewing an advertisement on the side of a bus, having a conversation with someone, walking, listening to the radio, bathing, visiting a new place, planting flowers, shopping for groceries, painting the fence, fishing, reading poetry, laughing at a grandchild fly a kite, attending a funeral, buying new shoes, shopping at a garage sale. "Anything can be a source for the next song. All this information – the ideas, pictures, thoughts, feelings, impressions – are stored in that computer up there, and somehow it noodles out as music. The craft of songwriting is knowing how to make something out of those bits and pieces. Life is my mentor. I am the apprentice."

Ideas, however, are fleeting and transient. Ideas are the bright, shiny and delicate jewels of inspiration that come quickly and repeatedly. Some people find it helpful to record the impressions, thoughts, sequences, words and chord combinations in a notebook, tape recorder or computer. Most songwriters don't 'hear' all at once. For some, lyrics come first; for others, it's melody or chord structure.

A songwriter's consciousness is life consciousness. A songwriter "thinks songs," taking those ideas and shaping them into something. What you communicate is your experience, feelings, perceptions and opinions. In an interview for *Guitar Player* magazine, September 1994, Johnny Cash recounts his experience in writing 'Folsom Prison Blues.' "I went to the movies at the base theater in 1953, and there was a movie called *Inside The Walls Of Folsom Prison*. It was a big movie during that time. I couldn't get it off my mind. I went back to my barracks, and I started writing lyrics. I don't remember what my first lines were. I'd just seen this movie and felt what it was like to be in prison through these prisoners and this story. I thought, 'I'm going to write this song as if I were a criminal. What could be the worst thing a criminal could do? Shoot a man just to watch him die.' That's where those lines came from. It came out of my head, but it was like some of the song I'd written about the farm. I wrote them as if I were there. A lot of people believed that I had been there. But it's like Merle Haggard said one time, 'Johnny Cash understands what it's like to be in prison, but he doesn't know.' "

In *Songwriters on Songwriting*, Jimmy Webb, one of Frank's favorite songwriters, recounts the story of writing 'MacArthur Park.' "I was living on Kirkwood Drive up on Laurel Canyon and I had just bought my first piano. I bought it with the royalties from 'Up, Up and Away.' It was my only possession. I had cushions under it so I ate under it and slept under it. (Laughs). Every once in a while I crawled out from under it and wrote something under it. So it's really my friend; it's really my good old friend. So I sat up for a couple of days and I experimented. I knew it needed movements. I knew that I wanted something very soaring that I would come back to at the end, and I put the basic thing together. As it turned out, the Association passed on it.

Frank's View

How to Write Better Songs

Write. If you're having trouble getting started, listen to music, dabble with some chords or just play on the keyboard. Just write whatever comes into your head. Don't worry about what it sounds like.

Write. Keep a notebook, journal or diary of your impressions or ideas. Or store them in your computer. Fill it with anything – ideas, images, thoughts, pieces of a song, lyrics. Song ideas, song titles and lyrics often come from this noodling around with tons of information we receive every day.

Write. Nobody has to see what you've written. Nobody will even care. But write because you have to.

Write. About what? The things listed at the beginning of this chapter. Things that bother you, excite you, frighten you, irritate you, upset you. Something or someone associated with a strong emotion may lead to a good song.

Write. Write a song about what you know or don't know. Write a song about your favorite dog, person, hobby. Write about things you hate or don't understand.

Write. Study the works of other songwriters. Try their style. Pretty soon you may find something that works for you.

Write. Regardless of how you feel, just write. Even if it's crap, write it anyways. Then put it away for a while. You don't have to look at it for a long time. You can edit yourself more objectively when you've had some distance. When you come back to the work after a while, you'll probably be amazed. The unexpected is a great teacher. You just might be surprised by your own writing.

Write. But don't forget to take a day off once in a while. Go out into the world. That's where the best songs come from. Life is more than writing. Rather, writing is really about life. Living is part of writing, too.

Write. Forget all the rules you've read. Find your own. Sometimes rules work, and sometimes they don't. Find what works for you.

Frank Mills

They didn't want to do it. And I had it in my trunk for a long time. In fact, it would have stayed in the trunk except that Richard Harris wanted to do it."

Creative people like Frank have the ability to absorb, digest and organize external stimuli, reshape them into something novel and communicate them in a musical art form. To some people, telephone touch tones are sounds heard when making a phone call. To a composer, they might become the basis of a melody that finds its way to a song. A combination of words overheard at the yacht club unravels the memory of an old love affair. A line of dialogue on a television program evokes happy childhood memories. Frank's music, and how he translates his experience of living, is a stream of musical thought that began around the Heintzman piano and will end when his ashes are scattered on the Bahamian waters, under the pine trees at Tremblant, and beneath the maples in Vermont.

Frank wrote 'Peter Piper,' (originally called 'Peter Piper Goes to Church') one of his earliest songs, for his nephew and godson, Ted Stone. His uncle was about 18 years old at the time and living with his sister Kathy and her husband Terry. Ted frequently sat on Frank's lap while he played.

'Somewhere a Child is Sleeping' was written in 1982 while he was living in New York with Trudy. Carol and Frank were divorcing and he was missing Jonathan. In 1992, Madeline Robertson, a friend from the Nassau Sailing Club, asked him if he could put words to what she thought was a Christmas song. Frank wrote the lyrics in four days so the choir could sing it in church Christmas morning.

'Chickadee' was written from experiences at Lac Tremblant. Sandra, annoyed by the chatter of the bird, used to say, "That darn bird wakes you up at 6 a.m." A flute plays the *chick-a-dee-dee*, the piano answers and then the song moves into a rolling monologue. Frank bought 20 plaster chickadees to promote the song. Three leftover black-capped chickadees, perched on the bookcase in the living room in Vermont, pay silent tribute to that pesky bird.

'Sketches of New England' was Frank's interpretation of the sea along the coast of New England.

Frank likens the song 'Island Hopping' to the bow scene in the movie *Titanic*. Leonardo DiCaprio, who plays the romantic hero Jack, a scrappy young artist traveling in steerage, embraces Kate Winslet who plays the unhappy upper-class Rose. The movie theme plays gently in the background as the doomed vessel cuts through the choppy, frigid water. Frank wrote his song while on a boating trip to Long Island. "It was a beautiful day, with azure water, the waves were dancing and all was right with the world. The boat was gently lulled in the arms of the sea."

The title for 'Let's Not Leave This Way' was reminiscent of a love affair gone sour.

'Storm Warning' was Frank's interpretation of Hurricane David which hit the Bahamas in 1979, shortly after the family's arrival.

'The Strawmarket Song' reflects Nassau's native shopping experience on downtown Bay Street, where tourists banter with colorful Bahamians for an armful of bargains in straw bags, hats, mats and novelty gifts, T-shirts, wood carvings and other souvenirs (that mostly come from Taiwan).

'Seascapes' is Frank's concept of a Debussy-like melody, reflecting the sea in her romantic mood.

Frank's faded, handwritten notes, found in the thick press clipping file in John Loweth's office, give the background on 'Rocky Mountain Sunrise,' written as a theme for a CBC television special. "One of the greatest moments in my life happened atop Windy Ridge in Alberta. To create a dramatic effect for the opening of the TV Special, *Rocky Mountain Christmas* (with yours truly), we helicoptered a white C-5 Yamaha grand piano to the summit of Windy Ridge. There I sat, alone except for mountain sheep, playing to the sun rising over the Rocky Mountains on a clear winters day. The camera crew in the 'copter were filming me playing 'Rocky Mountain Sunrise.' Knowing they couldn't hear what I was playing I burst into the chorale segment of Beethoven's Ninth Symphony. Heaven never seemed so near."

The same notes also give the background to 'The Traveler.' "Perhaps Achilles summed up the human dilemma best: 'To strive, to seek, to find but not to yield.' I recall saying good-bye to a man at Harbour Island, Bahamas. Alone, he would sail to the Azores and then on to Spain. 'The answer's in the searching,' he said. 'Always moving, always searching, that's the way of all the travelers. I'm a traveler and I'd best be on my way.' "

The background of 'Rose Island Days' is also listed in Frank's handwritten notes. "Oh, but the northern winters can be cold and long. It is a winter custom for Nassau town people to picnic on the endless white beaches of Rose Island. Whenever my travels find me caught in snowstorms and cold winter nights, 'Rose Island Days' is always on my mind."

Finding your own creative process

Every person who creates travels through the rhythms and realities of the creative process. The mind collects information, data, facts, ideas, opinions, impressions, thoughts, feelings, pictures, fantasies that serve as background or research for a creative project. The mind then links, blends, imagines, contrasts and connects this input into something. Over time, an artist must come to "know thyself" and how this creative work evolves. Some people work best in the morning, others in the evening, while some work best late at night. The point is, just do it. Work when you can for as long as you can. Take a break, then do something else. Discipline is developed when one sits at the keyboard, notebook, painting or whatever, working, day after day. You have to develop and understand your own routine of working.

"If you wait for inspiration to come before you write a song, you'll be waiting a long time. Do it. Write the song however it comes. You can always write it over again. Songs frequently happen while you're doing other things. With a songwriter's consciousness, you'll be aware and tuned in to those connections, insights, inspirations that are good material for a song. Discipline is an internal thing. Discipline, imposed upon another, is wrong. When discipline is self-imposed, it is a tool whereby we can grow, learn and push ourselves to our limits," recommends Frank.

Seemingly out of nowhere a new idea surfaces in Frank's mind to answer the creative challenge he faces. The next step is to write whatever his mind tells him. But to Frank, writing songs isn't orderly and systematically. Sometimes the ideas don't come, he gets stuck, he gets bored or he is tired. The other side of the soul is sometimes boring, uninspiring, devoid of novelty and originality. Creative work, otherwise known as toiling in the back-40, puts calluses on the hands, numbs the brain, leaves one drained, feeling exhausted and at times, totally frustrated. The creative act follows the nature of life, quickening, birth, rising energy to a zenith, and then atrophy, decline and death. The act of creating becomes, as Byron described it in "Childe Harold's Pilgrimage," essential in its own right:

> 'Tis to create, and in creating live
> A being more intense, that we endow
> With form our fancy, gaining as we give
> The life we image, even as I do now.
> What am I? Nothing; but no so art thou,
> Soul of my thought! with whom I traverse earth,
> Invisible but grazing, as I glow
> Mix'd with thy spirit, blending with thy birth,
> And feeling still with thee in my crush'd feeling's dearth.

Writer's block is a common concern among artists of all sorts. Frank has his own way of overcoming the problem. "When I get stuck, I do something else. I have several different songs going on all the time. I don't always finish one before I start another. I'll go fishing, work in the garden, or go to the sailing club. Before I've even got the worm on the line I've got the answer to that problem. The problem always works itself out. If I try too hard and force it, it doesn't come. When I'm doing other things besides songwriting that's where some of my best ideas come from. But I still have to work at writing songs. It just doesn't happen."

Carole King, writer of 'Will You Love Me Tomorrow,' 'It's Too Late,' and 'You've Got a Friend,' offers a few suggestions on overcoming writer's block in *Songwriters on Songwriting*: "Songwriters, both lyricists and melody writers, are often plagued with the thing most often known as writer's block. All songwriters are writers of prose as well. I have found that the key to not having blocks is to not worry about it. Ever.

"If you are sitting down and you feel that you want to write and nothing is coming, you get up and do something else. Then you come back and try it again. But you do it in a relaxed manner. Trust that it will be there. If it ever was once, and you've ever done it once, it will be back. It always comes back and the only thing that is a problem is when you get in your own way worrying about it.

"I'd like to say that I almost never have worried about it. Because when it seemed to be a problem, when I seemed to be...I don't even want to say blocked, because it seems like too strong a word. But when the channel wasn't open enough to let something through, I always went and did something else and never worried about it and it always opened up again. Whether it was an hour later, which is often the case, or a day or a week later, or sometimes a few months later, I just didn't worry about it."

Frank summarizes his understanding of songwriting: "If you want to be a songwriter, write songs. An intense understanding of life is needed to write great songs. Numb people don't write songs. You can't write a song when you're numb because when you're in that state you're not alive. You have to have died to live. You have to have failed to win. You have to have experienced life to write about it."

9

SOUNDING THE SOUL

WANTED: POET OF THE MUNDANE. Must be able to put forth in interesting ways things that people normally don't express. Must be able to describe the monotonous, sameness, ordinariness and everydayness of life in creative, unusual ways. Must be able to document life's haunting uncertainties and struggles, its ironies and absurdities and its brave possibilities. Must be willing to take intellectual and emotional risks. Must be able to make up his own mind about things. Must be a rebel. Must like to have fun and frequently try new things. Must battle boredom. Must be a daydreamer who gets totally lost in a fantasy and becomes oblivious to everything else. Must be able to see complex relationships between seemingly unrelated situations or ideas. Must be self-motivated, preserving and passionate about sounding the soul. Numb people need not apply.

Frank never applied for the position. It came with the cards he was dealt. His hand was the "mind of sound." Frank arrived at the poker table of life with fanaticism and an extraordinary relationship to sound, with songwriting talent, a multi-faceted personality, a huge dose of creativity, a knack for mechanical things, and an ordered, both-feet-on-the-floor approach to business. The wild cards were his personality, re-occurrences of his father's anger, the slings and arrows of the music business and the inherent, chaos of creativity itself.

"There doesn't seem to be much evidence that I inherited my father's problems with heart disease and cancer. Not yet. Maybe I have been spared those genes that destroyed him. We all get a deck of cards and some of us are luckier than others. I got a good dose of latent music talent that had to be awakened. Nobody knew how far it would go. I also got talents with business and mechanical things. There seems to be a mix of talents with not too much focus in one area. A Beethoven I'm not. I'm what you could call a "normal" musician. Mozart, who had a genius for music but not much else, appears to have been a raving lunatic. The same with Beethoven. Bach was perhaps one of the "normal" musicians. He wrote and performed most of his music as an organist in a church," reflects Frank.

For Frank, an event is a complex opera of sound, a major medium in which he perceives life. It is sound that shapes, expresses and makes sense of his daily pleasures, lingering doubts and unanswered questions. To this musician, sound is security, a navigation system, a way of seeing, and a way of making sense and meaning. Painters and sculptors are nourished by light and color. Frank knows life when he hears it. He eats sound. "My ears are like two gamma ray machines. They suck up sound. It's an intuitive awareness of my surroundings, my environment."

Call it his "symphony of place." To many people, weather is something they see on TV or hear on the radio. Frank lives by rain, snow, heat, cold and storms. "A barometer is very important to me. I need to know what's going on around me." Seaman Frank is like a wild creature whose ears, eyes and nostrils are continually moving, testing its surroundings for the approach of prey, predators or an upheaval. First the calm. Then just enough wind to tickle the leaves on the trees. Powerful gusts follow. The maples sway, their upper branches massaging those below. The sky darkens, sometimes to a navy black, other times to a rich purple. Weather, quickly and intensely, can transform in a few hours the playground in which he relaxes, to a grim arena in which he struggles for life. Like the sea, weather hikes his hopes and withers his prospects. The sight of the coast fills him with gladness or with terror.

Eskimos call this special sensitivity to sound *seuketat*, "the ear of the animal." While others may only hear a sound, in the crashing and clanking of dishes, bits of conversation, bicycle horns and chirping sparrows, Frank easily detects subtle distinctions, picking up timbre, overtones, harmonies, pitches, emotions and counterpoints. At 7 a.m., he needs to identify the noise outside the window, "Is that *whirr whirrrr whirrrrrr* the garbage truck or something that will kill me?"

The purr of working appliances – the *plunk, drip, plunk, rrrhurr* of the ice-maker, the *er, er, errrrr* of the ceiling fan, and the gentle *tic, tic, tic*, of the alarm clock – soothes his disturbed slumber. Some 100 feet away he hears the *fizz, fizz, fusselll* of a champagne bottle opening. In his sugarbush, where numerous sounds compete for attention, he points out that the *clink, clack, gurr, clunk* is the water heater gurgling some 300 feet away.

Frank's musical neurology manifests itself as delicate sensitivity to sound. Loud music, rock music and rap music are uncomfortable to him. The hahrang – chatter, screeching, yelling – of children is sometimes disturbing. As an infant Mozart became sick by loud sounds. Mendelssohn cried whenever he heard music. "This music! It is here in my head. Save me from it," wailed the young Tchaikovsky. Handel would not enter a concert hall until the instruments had been tuned. Bach flew into a rage upon hearing wrong notes.

Howard Gardner is his book *Frames of Mind* states there are seven levels of intelligence. While everyone has a combination of all seven, most people are usually dominant in one or two areas.

* Verbal/linguistic: the ability to manipulate words in their oral or written form.
* Mathematical/logical: the ability to manipulate number systems and logical concepts.
* Spatial: the ability to see and manipulate patterns and designs.
* Musical: the ability to understand and manipulate musical concepts such as tone, rhythm, and harmony.
* Bodily-kinesthetic: the ability to use one's body and movement, such as in sports and dance.
* Intrapersonal: the ability to understand one's feelings and to be reflective and philosophical.

* Interpersonal: the ability to understand other people and their thoughts and feelings.

As a thinker in sound, making something out of nothing is the special province of Frank's musical intelligence. Frank creates music by "hearing it out." That is, his "mind's ear," his memory and imagination are rich and strong in vivid tonal imagery. He can build the most complex musical structures and hear and feel all the effects of every detailed element before he has written down a note or sounded it out by voice or instrument. Like a storyteller scans his world for ideas, this composer navigates the hierarchy of categories, plucking ideas and combining them into musical figures and phrases, cadences and whole compositions. As the storyteller knows of people and places, Frank knows the music of Mozart, Wagner, Beethoven, Clapton, Charles to Rachmaninoff. In some aspects, his mind resembles a chess masters. He carries around a huge library of musical patterns that can be combined in myriad ways to produce his style of compositions. Take out the image from the musical mind and you take out its very essence. Imagery at a deeper level is "felt" more than "heard."

Mozart had visions of sound. He heard music in his head. Whether he was performing his own pieces, seated at the composition table, conducting, or listening to others, he continually reconfigured the musical visions in his mind. Beethoven saw musical notes in his head. "I'm not Beethoven but I do have much in common with him. He could look at a sheet of music and hear it playing in his head. When I see a sheet of music I hear the orchestra playing as vividly as if it were in front of me. I can hear it when they turn up the bassoons, the violins or the clarinets," says Frank.

Frank's musical ability manifests itself most strongly in his gift of melody. His gift was enhanced studying composition with Istvan Anhalt at McGill. With The Bells he had to compete with two electric guitars, an acoustic guitar, an electric bass and a drum. In self-defense he played high on the keyboard. It was the only place he could hear himself.

Frank also has the ability to hear and remember strong melodies in his head. Many songwriters and composers record inspired moments in notebooks. Before acquiring his MIDI system, Frank rarely wrote anything down. Now he writes those melodies and stores them in his computer. The melody usually comes to him in strong, memorable form. Without a strong melody there is no meaning to the song. If he can't recall the melody, the song probably wasn't supposed to be written.

Speaking about Frank's melodic gifts, Michael Hoppe describes his friend as a highly skilled carpenter who can carve the chair the right way and make it graceful and attractive. "With Frank, you have a sense of distinctiveness, a clarity, sense of musical focus and completion. There is no noodling," says Hoppe. Mozart said that melody is a series of notes that have to kiss each other. Like a line drawing, melody has a distinctive form and shape. Frank hears music through his eyes. You can't learn how to design these notes in school or on a computer. They are felt, deep within the soul of the composer. While the skill of writing melodies can be enhanced, it's extremely difficult to learn. "It's a feeling, a gift. You either have it or you don't."

Something happens when we listen, not only to Frank's music, but to any artist. Music is a paradox. It is a peacemaker of sorts. It softens and opens hearts. But it is also an enchanter that transmutes the sullen irritability, anger, frustration and unrest that sometimes seethes in the soul. It calms the overwrought human mind and rouses it just as effectively. Sound rises, moves, ebbs and splashes as feelings do. Music sounds the way emotions feel. Music remains to the receptive soul a passionate communication of feelings too deep for words, "a cry from heart to heart," said Tchaikovsky.

Artistic, creative types like Frank operate in the realm of intuition, feeling, imagination, ideas and inspiration. In 1987, Frank took a professional development aptitude test based on the Kolbe Conative System. Not surprisingly, it showed a more accurate picture of his talents than the report at Union Carbide. The Kolbe Conative System measures preferences in four modes; fact finder, follow through, quick start, implementor. Nobody is all of any single mode. Rather, everyone has a profile of all modes. Individuals usually possess a dominance in one mode, indicating their preferred modus operandi or method of operation. Through the fact finder mode individuals are pragmatist, prober, arbitrator, practitioner, researcher, judge or realist. In the follow through mode individuals are planner, designer, regulator, theorist, programmer, systematizer, pattern maker. Catalyst, generalist, innovator, entrepreneur, promoter and impressionist characterize the quick start mode. Individuals operate in implementor mode as manufacturer, molder, builder, athlete, agriculturist, handler.

He scored 15 percent on follow through, 25 percent on the fact finder, and 30 percent each on quick start and implementor. This test indicates that

Frank is most productive when he innovates, initiates, promotes, demonstrates, constructs, masters, invents, brainstorms, originates, crafts, repairs, displays, devises, challenges, contrives, builds, practices, renders, risks, changes, reforms, fixes, forms, improvises, plays hunches, experiments, holds, shapes, puts together and uses physical effort. Resistance comes in having to tackle tasks with structure, routine, precision or efficiency or by designing a system, following guidelines, making a plan or being tidy.

As an intuitive-type, Frank sees things in terms of meanings, relationships and possibilities that go beyond the information obtained from the here-and-now, facts and logic. Buckminster Fuller described intuition as cosmic fishing: "Once you feel a nibble, you've got to hook the fish." Intuition consists of sudden thoughts, the flashes of ideas that usually arrive in the mind instantaneously, moving so quickly it's difficult to catch them. For Frank, sudden thoughts occur while fishing, taking a shower, driving a car, at 3 a.m., or in the sugarbush. Sometimes glimpses comes as a "nagging" feeling. Other times, there are images – fully fleshed out, vivid, colorful, or sketches or blurs – and pictures that pop into his mind with no obvious origin. Gut feelings, distinctive uncomfortable physical sensations relay a message. Strong flashes of emotion are often related to a situation, issue, or a person he's just met. They could be positive feelings that draw him to someone or something or negative impulses that warn him to stay away.

An effervescent curiosity, a need to know and a need to create keep Frank moving from quantum physics to classical mechanics to cigar rolling to laser surgery to barometers to piano tuning to making jam to growing potatoes to growing tomatoes to pickling beets to astronomy to bird calls to ice fishing to the *Celestine Prophecy* to alternative medicine to the *Perfect Storm* to tides to global positioning to electronics to air conditioning to plumbing to fire works to welding to skiing to theology to flying to stocks to mutual funds to economics to flyfishing to night-blooming jasmine to kites to trailer hitches to evaporators. Like a junkie, he has an insatiable need to see things, to discover first-hand the magic, paradoxical truth and tragedy of life. He calls this "living above mundanity." His hunger wants to taste something fresh, to express life's ordinary moments in different ways.

A sense of gratitude and generosity comes out of his love of life. Frank assists three needy families in Nassau on a weekly basis, contributes to the Salvation Army, is a member of the St. Andrew Society (a charity that helps the elderly and ill), is a life member of the Bahamas National Trust and a member of the Bahamas Air-Sea Rescue Association. Over the years he has played at various charity functions including Toronto Sick Children's Hospital, the Canadian Cancer Society, and numerous telethons. He is presently the honorary chairperson of the Owen Sound Theatre Refurbishing Committee, a committee established to restore an historic theatre in Owen Sound, Ontario. Frank has established a scholarship fund at McGill University and is a significant contributor to the institution's 21st Century Fund.

He states that his greatest gift is the ability to feel things more intensely than other people. "The intensity is the gift. The intensity of living each moment. The ability to see things, to be open to experience and try new combinations. This challenges your thinking and expands your horizons," says Frank. "It's a talent to look at something and wonder what makes it tick, to become totally involved with it, to "live" it. You can't own a boat without knowing how to change a fuel filter or what makes the generator run. I've got to get in there and fix it myself. Through this curiosity and intensity comes a sheer reverence for life.

"I liken it to Zorba the Greek. It is the sum of the child in me, the glory of life and this marvelous opportunity we have." In Nikos Kazantzakis's book *Zorba the Greek*, set on the Greek isle of Crete, Basil, a shy inhibited writer from England is befriended by Zorba, a boisterous, gregarious peasant with an astonishing love of life. When Zorba agrees to work at Basil's abandoned mine, it is the beginning of a lesson for the young man as he gradually moves from an observer of the world to a participant. After spending several weeks with Zorba, Basil comes to the conclusion ..."Yes, I understood. Zorba was the man I had sought so long in vain. A living heart, a large voracious mouth, a great brute soul, not yet severed from mother earth. The meaning of the words, art, love, beauty, purity, passion, all this was made clear to me by the simplest of words uttered by this workman."

It's not surprising that Frank reacts so strongly to numb people and people who live small lives. "To life, to live! That's what it's all about. It bothers me that some people live such small lives. They live in the same town all their lives. They go to work, go home and then watch TV on Saturday night. They do that every week. Their world is small, boring. I would find it extremely difficult and very painful to survive like that," says Frank.

Frank rarely visits what he calls the numb side of Nassau. Travel brochures claim Paradise Island is the "real Bahamas." Slot machines, craps, roulette, baccarat, Big Six wheels, Caribbean stud poker, fabricated beaches and aquariums cater to tourists seeking a once-in-a-lifetime, get-away-from-it-all vacation. "What's so exciting about sitting at a stupid slot machine and losing all that money? It's numb, numb, numb. This isn't the "real" Bahamas; it's artificial, made-up, manufactured." For Frank, the real Bahamas is sailing for three or four days on choppy, open waters to an antiquated island, snorkeling for grouper, watching starfish in moonlight crawl across the white ocean floor or avoiding the jaws of 'the man in the grey flannel suit.'

Several years ago, Frank took a 10-day cruise to Alaska aboard a luxury cruise liner. On these cruises, passengers are at sea almost as much as they are on shore. Numerous onboard activities such as eating, movies, casinos, suntanning, and nightlife, keep the tourists occupied until the next shore excursion. Frank was quite perturbed at the whole affair. "People save up all their lives to stand in line for breakfast with 500 other people? That's not my idea of fun." For him, real Alaska is watching a black bear flipping boulders like flapjacks, watching sparkles of water flash off a just-caught trout, bald eagles, aloof and silent as gargoyles preparing to hunt, and inhaling the fragrance of oysters, snapping and sizzling over an open fire.

"It's part of the package. Intensity combined with a love of experience. Whatever I do, I try to do it intensely, whether that's navigation, music, loving, sugarin', spearfishing, running...whatever. I'd like my epitaph to say, 'I came and I did it and I did everything I could.' "

Call it need, drive, passion, purpose, desire, dream or obsession. Within Frank, as with most every composer, there is something that compels him to "create," for only the act of creation can truly satiate his spiritual craving. Music fills a need that no lover, child, material possession or religion can satisfy. For Frank, writing music is more than a form of artistic expression. There is an insatiable need to sound the soul, to search passionately for expression and language adequate to the pleasures and pains of his experience of life. There are disturbing silences between the sounds. Sometimes, it is more than his spirit can stand. When words are inadequate, meaningless, and physical gestures fall short, music is a language by which his heart speaks. It is his definition of being alive.

Soul has to do with genuineness and depth, as when we say certain music has soul or a remarkable person is soulful. Sounding the soul speaks to the longings we feel and to the symptoms that distress us. A soulful personality is sometimes complicated, multi-faceted, and shaped by both pain and pleasure, uncertainty and possibility, doubt and faith. Soul is a dimension of experiencing life and ourselves. In some individuals, like Frank, intensity tends to accompany soulful living. A passionate, erratic and often unpredictable emotional makeup is part of his artistic temperament. Bach hurled his wig at fumbling musicians. Handel once lobbed a kettledrum across the stage. Beethoven returned food to the restaurant kitchen via the waiter's head. Chopin once broke a chair in response to an unfortunate student's playing. Mahler railed from the conductor's podium so often that he regularly declined duel challenges from the players.

For such is Frank's life, a storm whereon he must ride. He likens his emotional experience to Irving Stone's book *The Agony and the Ecstasy*, which follows Michelangelo, the tortured artist through the unpredictable creative process. "I look at my own past that way. There were moments of the highest ecstasy and moments of the deepest agony. The high parts are very visible to others. The agony you do alone."

Frank relates Michelangelo's sculptor/painter struggle to his songwriter and pianist syndrome. The artist was distraught, even destroying his works, when commissioned to paint the Sistine Chapel. He considered himself a sculptor, not a painter. "I think I did my best work locked in my studio writing, not traveling the world playing the piano. Someone once said nothing much culturally was ever accomplished by nomads. They spend too much time dealing with survival. I don't consider myself a piano player. When people ask 'what do you do for a living?' I say 'I'm a songwriter.' I never say 'piano player.' I've had to play piano, that was part of the package, but I'm a songwriter. There are guys in the classics who could play circles around me, anytime. But then, I'm not competing with them. It's like saying, 'Garth Brooks isn't competing with Pavarotti. And that's the business.' "

While a little emotional wobble makes for good music, the intensity has also produced some of his deepest regrets. When Frank was young and full of ragery, he would frequently erupt in uncontrollable anger. Like his father, an accumulation of things ignited the episode. Carole, Nancy, Jonathan, Sandra and Trudy were on the receiving end of an avalanche, a mountain of regret, rage, heartache, betrayal that left everyone else in ruins.

"Dad wasn't easy to live with. He always had that temper. He would freak. As a child, I was absolutely terrified of him. He'd get a beet red face and he'd run after me. One time, he chased me up the stairs and I hide in the closet. He pulled me out of the closet and spanked me. Mom was saying 'stop, stop, don't do that,' " remembers Sandra.

Nancy recollects her Dad as a volcano ready to erupt. "He had a violent temper. He was under extreme pressure. He had those fits of anger. For 10 years it wasn't always a picnic." The outbursts were dubbed "peaks."

Jonathan remembers watching the pressure build, "It was an accumulation of things. The garbage didn't get picked up, there'd be something wrong with the boat or whatever. Then a pin would drop and everything would come out. It never seemed to be about us or directed at us but I knew after a while that it was just a buildup of everything."

Friends and business associates recall Frank as being an angry, volatile young man. John Loweth, his business partner, watched and listened to him rail over unsold records, mistakes on tour details, missed deadlines and a host of other happenings in business. John also says that these angry outbursts have calmed considerably over the years.

Michael Hoppe saw a struggling musician: "He was bursting to be successful but he didn't know how. His marriage wasn't happy. When he did become successful, former frustrations erupted. Then his marriage ended and Frank got very, very angry. He showed an enormous wrath, obviously pent-up from years of disappointment. I knew it wasn't directed at me personally but at a number of things. He had this deep, deep rage. He went completely ballistic."

Psychiatric sessions after Trudy left helped to gain some perspective and calm the raging storm. Today, he is a calmer, more peaceful and grateful man. Friends, family and business associates agree that Frank is calmer and relaxed. His peaks are infrequent. "He is softer. I think that as he's gotten older he's learned to deal with more things. Things don't bother him as much as they used to," says Nancy.

Frank comments on the change. "I was a hell of a father to live with. I deeply regret that. I think that as I've gotten older I've mellowed. I understand myself better. It's also another time. Ambition isn't there anymore. I'm not a charging moose at an airline ticket counter yelling at the attendant about the late plane. I've learned that I have my checks and balances. My touch of high blood pressure can flare up if I don't take my medication. I know I'm going to be in trouble if I don't exercise. I've always had this need for calmness and beautiful environments. My peaceful homes in Stowe, Tremblant and Nassau help to quiet the storm."

While there were many tears and anger growing up with their Dad, there was much laughter. "He's fascinating, curious, fun. He's a real nut. We used to laugh so hard," says Sandra. Peter Batson and Michael Hoppe both call him a "red-necked mimic." With a fondness for dialects, Frank is renowned for his impersonations of native Indians, Scots, Bahamians and Captain Highliner. "Ach, ach. Pipers for Charrlee saakkee. Marches, parrradddes, pipers, festivals. All the good things in life, which err generation has nor appreciation fer," is his Scotticism.

One of his favorite western movies is *The Outlaw Josey Wales* starring Clint Eastwood and Chief Dan George, who gives a performance that is comical and marvelously dignified as the Indian who, though he can't even sneak up on a white man, proudly claims, 'I never surrendered.' When Frank is driving his tractor in Vermont, barbecuing on the patio at his home in Nassau or Vermont, riding in the van with band members, he slips into his gruff, baritone, Chief Dan George impersonation: "Hmmmm....my people...hmmmm ...my people." "It's pretty hard to sneak up on an Indian." "You want to eat, hmmm." "Let's go back to the teepee and eat. My wife cooks pretty good dog."

That which emanates from Frank is often not conscious willpower or even a planned purpose. It is the sheer force of life, a voltage. Inspiration and songwriting is not conjured up. It comes as a gift, from somewhere, someone, outside himself. The ideas, the melodies, the images, that forward creation, that bring form to potential, "visit" him. He does not make them, entertain them in a hospitable context, debate them or judge them. The creative act comes unbidden as something other than self. At times, this pull, this tug, this mission to realize the possibility to create, becomes his master. In its service, Frank may lose track of time, forget about others and even forget to eat or sleep. In an act of courage, not knowing why or how an inspiration – or a song – will turn out, he throws himself into it, heart and soul.

While many people pay tribute to the products of creation – books, songs, paintings, mathematical formulas, art, buildings – the artist becomes, at times against his will, like a madman, trying to understand the paradoxical nature of the creative process. Creativity goes beyond man's tidy, controlled and largely false world. While creative work can be exciting, inspiring and godlike, it is also humdrum, full of anxieties, mistakes and failures. It is not some easy-to-build, paint-by-number formula. The creative act has been called a magician, masquerading as a friend and trusted advisor, a slayer of the real, a trickster, a mischievous maker and weaver of illusions.

Being called to the creative life means being able to stand the fires, droughts, desires and passions. The creative act pits the creator against the uncreated, against the sheer compulsion to make something new, an unheard sound, an image never imagined, an untried solution. It asks families and friends close to the creator to accept him, perhaps without understanding and getting hurt in the process. Some people think that it takes a strange mind to hear the sounds of wind and water, birdsong and human cries and collect, shape, organize and put them into some order. The composer has often been cast as a tragic hero, misunderstood, disdained in his time and poor as a church mouse. He must throw himself into all the exotic, passionate, unconventional experiences he can, tasting the "forbidden fruits" so that he can learn the secrets of the human soul. An artist ought to be a bit bizarre. Many artists may feel compelled to portray the image of the mad genius or radical to increase their public appeal.

The creative dilemma and the image problem have been ongoing sources of frustration for Frank. "It's hard to define me, an instrumental artist. To some people I'm dull and boring. There is this side of me that is creative. But there is also this side of me that is business-like. The cards I got were 50 percent music and 50 percent business. I've met many artistic, creative people who got about 98 percent music and about two percent business. They are the 'I'm dedicated to my ax (my music) kind of people.' "

In showbiz, that translates to nothing to talk about. "I'm a middle-aged, suburbia-type guy, who looks like somebody's father. That ain't gonna sell music videos. The media found it hard to grasp onto anything about me as a person. Bob Dylan? Look out. You don't know what he's going to do. He might take his clothes off. People who are successful with the press tend to have this kind of image. I'm just a normal guy. Some musicians I have met are so obsessed with music. All they know and talk about is music. It's them and "their ax." While music is a part of life, it's not all there is. Music is a small part of all the things I do to enjoy life. Life is my profession, music is my hobby."

In 1984 Frank read the book *The Demise of the Instrumental in the North American Music Industry*. In some ways he can relate to that. "I've never been part of the hoopla, fast-paced promo of rock 'n' roll and heavy metal. It's always been a struggle to get press and publicity. My hair isn't spiked and purple and I don't have five earrings and I don't swear all the time." Only once in his career did the media find a radical composer image. In an early '80s interview, when Frank had grown a beard, the newspaper printed a bad photograph. "Anybody in his right mind could see that it was just terrible. I looked awful. But here I was supposed to be the fanatical 'artist.' "

Frank says his life parallels the lyrics and imagery in Jimmy Webb's song 'Dancing Girl,' performed by Richard Harris on the album *A Tramp Shining*. In that song an old man dances with his girl until his dreams come true. In the background, the music continues to play. He knows that the show will once again steal his hopes for love. Webb sums up the song and the old man's life:

> *"When the curtain calls and it will I know you will leave my arms*
> *and go on with the show*
> *I know and it will be a lonely world without you dancing girl*
> *Oh my love, I'll miss you so."*

"On that album an old man is reminiscing about what could have been. Which says a lot about me and the music business. The music business discards. The "show" becomes the ultimate thing. Some musicians will tell you they have more fun playing than dealing with a wife and three kids at home. Is it any wonder that musicians have a higher rate of divorce, suicide and drug abuse? Families play second fiddle to the obsession," reflects Frank.

This man has always struggled with the inner turmoil of being an artist. "It is such a big part of you. You're born with this and it's something you can't change even if you wanted to. Hopefully, you can allow yourself the luxury of a normal life. Music is so great, so easy and so much fun. It's part of your soul. It's all encompassing. There is the elation of arranging songs, these wonderful crossword puzzles that they are. It's your soul, your guts, your heart pouring these things out. This wonderful thing comes and visits you. God knows from where it comes, from somewhere deep, deep, down. There are times when I'd sooner be playing my piano than doing anything else. When things get tough I play. Here is this thing, this marvelous creation of yours that you worship and you can't help but do. You can't give it up for anything. It is a passion that can be all consuming."

The gift, however, comes with conflict and difficulties. Sometimes, the family is sacrificed on the alter of ambition. "When families are supposed to be having supper, a musician is driving to a gig. Showbiz is at such odds with the nine to five work pattern. Our work starts when the office is closed. We play evenings when the kids have a football or soccer game. We play 24 hours except when we are sleeping."

Frank's deepest regrets concern his family and personal relationships. "I would like to have said, 'I was a devoted family man.' I wasn't. It didn't happen. I also have regrets that women I've been involved with haven't understood the tugging. It is such a glorious profession, but there is a price to pay. Sorrow is joy's constant companion."

EPILOGUE

At times, his life was a raging storm.

Perhaps he fell in love too many times, too quickly and not too wisely.

He did not always treat those who loved him or were devoted to him with love, care and respect.

His rages were injurious. Today, he's a much calmer, grateful man.

There is melancholy and sadness in the knowledge that all things past will continue unchanged.

There is hope for a new dawn rising in the sugarbush.

There were happy endings. Other endings were bitter, painful disappointments.

There are songs that will never be sung.

There are many songs left to write.

He loves to fly kites with his three grandsons who call him "Grumps."

Some fences will never be mended. New ones have been erected.

Like Dorothy in the Wizard of Oz, he found a great deal of adventure in his backyard, but at other times, lost the red shoes.

He set a place for an unexpected guest.

He risked change to believe in tomorrow.

He loved, he lived, he wrote, he did most of it – like Zorba the Greek.

The sound of his spirit will last until the game is called on account of darkness.

He captured the sound of chickadees, heartache, seascapes, broken dreams, passion – life music.

He didn't become a doctor of medicine. He is a doctor of the soul.

He regrets not having written with Mack David. He can still write film scores.

Like fairy tales, his songs bring order out of inner chaos, both his and those of the listener, by revealing the hidden meanings of life's lessons at a pace the listener can accept.

He makes no apologies for his strong opinions.

He mistrusts big government and ambition-stifling over-taxation.

He boasts of being a backporch realist.

He tunes his own piano. He can recognize a piano in distress from a mile away.

His favorite color is blue – especially the gin-clear blue of the Bahamian waters.

He had setbacks and struggles. He accepted many of them. Others he may never get over. Music is a regular medicine to heal those wounds.

He likes humanity in small doses.

He craves peace and quiet.

He rolls his own Cuban cigars.

His favorite kind of pie is pumpkin.

Songs are chapters in his life. They are his autobiography.

He wrote music about love, laughter, pain, misery, joy, gladness.

A craftsman earns his keep through his expertise. This artist invented his job.

Sounding the soul lead to places he didn't know, to places he sought in the very beginning, to places he didn't know existed but later discovered in his own world – his own heart.

Some regrets are deeper than the Bahama Bank.

The many scalding tears he's cried have burnt small holes in his face. The invisible scares are there, like pinpricks or small pox, and have never faded.

But the poker game must acknowledge the other wild card – life itself. For as long as he's stayed in the game, life's surprises, challenges and catastrophes have influenced every move he made. "Fortune has allowed me the luxury of capitalizing on the music cards I got. Life has been extremely good to me, for which I shall be eternally grateful. That's my contract with God – gratitude."

He is a salt, a dreamer, a creator, an imaginative soul, who brought back with him words and sounds and images to describe mundanity.

As an artist on a voyage, his moods are often his ships of passage.

The sea is yet another voyage, with its many keys, moods, tauntings, adventures and tragedies.

Music is the cry he utters, the balm that soothes his fears.

He made some bad choices. He made lots of mistakes.

He hurt people. People hurt him.

In some aspects, his life was a plot beyond his own devising, binding him like Judas in grief and guilt and betrayal. It's difficult to say exactly where his suffering begins and his complexity ends.

No one will ever know what would have happened if he had taken a different route. Whatever the personal toll of the quest, it would have been a tragedy to have fallen short of his dreams, or even worse, to have never dreamed at all.

If only destiny were as easy as picking up a green marble, or a robin's egg, a trinket, a locket or a toy – we could see it in the palm of the hand.

Like a blacksmith, he bent red iron in the smithy, like a wordsmith, he struggled with words and meanings – his smithy of the soul is words, sounds, keys, pitches, harmony.

Perhaps Frankie's words, scribbled between the writing of Shakespeare, Keats, Wordsworth, Shelley and Melville in his grade eight workbook, say it best. Long before he could see ahead, he wrote the key to seeing his future: *"I still have my God, my sounds and my soul."*

Frank Mills Discography

Singles

1972	Love Me, Love Me, Love
1972	Poor Little Fool
1972	Sunshine Morning
1972	Reflections of my Childhood
1973	How can I be Sure
1976	Look at me Real
1976	When Summer is Gone
1978	Music Box Dancer
1979	Peter Piper
1979	Most People are Nice
1980	Breakaway
1981	Happy Song
1981	Plaisir D'Amour

Albums

1971 ***Seven of my Songs (Plus Some Others)***

1972 ***Reflections of my Childhood***

1973 ***Frank Mills and his Orchestra***
(re-released in 1978 as ***The Poet and I***)

1976 ***Look at me Real*** (The Canadian Talent Library)

1978 ***The Poet and I***

1978 ***Music Box Dancer***
Music Box Dancer • From a Sidewalk Cafe • Theme from the Silver Broom • When you Smile • Love's Like That • Storm Warning • The Poet and I • Spanish Coffee • You Don't Love no More • Valse Classique • 401 West • Music Box Dancer

1979 ***Sunday Morning Suite***

Sunday Morning Suite • Peter Piper • Most People are Nice • Wherever You Go • On the Move • Reflections • Piano Lesson #5 • Mary, Queen of Scots • Interlude • The Happy Song • Ski Fever

1981 ***Prelude to Romance***

Prelude to Romance (Part 1) • Smile • Try to Remember • Yesterday When I was Young • Without you • Spanish Love Song • Anticipation • Prelude to Romance (Part 11) • Send in the Clowns • Plaisir D'Amour • September Song • Moulin Rouge • Somewhere a Child is Sleeping • Prelude to Romance

1982 ***Rondo***

Chickadee • A Mind of her Own • Are you Still Loving me? • He's Alright • Rondo in America • A Classical Rock • A Song for Andromeda • Concerto No. 1 for Piano • Rock Band and Orchestra • 1 First Movement, Adante • 11 Second Movement, Adagio • 111 Third Movement, Allegro

1983 ***Frank Mills, A Special Christmas***

Fanfare/Joy to the World • Good King Wenceslas • Oh Little Town of Bethlehem • What Child is This? • Oh Holy Night • God Rest ye Merry Gentlemen • Oh Come all ye Faithful • Cathedral Bells are Ringing • It Came Upon a Midnight Clear • Oh Christmas Tree • The First Noel • We Three Kings • Silent Night • Hark the Herald Angels Sing

1985 ***The Traveler***

Rocky Mountain Sunrise • The Traveler • Mariachi Festival • A Song for Haruko • Just Foolin' Around • The Streets of Tel Aviv • Rose Island Days • One Vienna Night • Sadness is Goodbye • Moving On

1986 ***Transitions***

Heart of the City • Seascapes • Sketches of New England • Shadows of the Dancer • Signs of Conflict • Diamond in the Rough • Island Hopping • Let's not Leave This Way • Storm Warning • Transitions and Triumphs

1987 ***Over Sixty Minutes with Frank Mills***

Music Box Dancer • Storm Warning • The Poet and I • Sunday Morning Suite • Peter Piper • Piano Lesson # 5 • Ski Fever • A Spanish Love Song • Prelude to Romance • Rondo in America • A Classical Rock • Concerto No. 1 for Piano • The Traveler • Rose Island Days • One Vienna Night • Moving On

1988 ***My Piano***

That Crazy Little Piano Song • If you Loved Me • When we're Dancing • Kitty on the Keys • The Blues Don't Last • Tocatta Amerasia • Save it for Tomorrow • Piano Fun • The Strawmarket Song • Largo • Riding High

1989 ***The Twentieth Anniversary Album***

Music Box Dancer • From a Sidewalk Cafe • The Poet and I • Sunday Morning Suite • Peter Piper • Piano Lesson #5 • Prelude to Romance • Terms of Endearment • Theme from Moulin Rouge • Send in the Clowns • Islands in the Stream • Yesterday, When I was Young • Smile • Kitty on the Keys • The Blues Don't Last • A Classical Rock • Concerto #1, 2, 3 • Heart of the City • Together Through the Years

1991 ***Gather Round the Piano with Frank Mills & Friends***

Hail, Hail the Gang's all Here • Take me out to the Ballgame • The Old Lamplighter • Edelweiss • Beer Barrel Polka • Beautiful Brown Eyes • Amazing Grace • Let the Rest of the World go by • She'll be Coming Round the Mountain • Molly Malone • Red Sails in the Sunset • Shenandoah • I'm Looking Over a Four Leaf Clover • Sloop John B • Home on the Range • Bells of St. Mary • You are my Sunshine • Whispering Hope • The Traveler • Now is the Hour • Yellow Rose of Texas • Goodnight Irene

1993 ***Happy Music***

Music Box Dancer • Frank's Rag • Seascapes • Chickadee • Prelude to Romance • Peter Piper • Ski Fever • Piano Lesson #5 • The Poet and I • Happy Song • Sunday Morning Suite • Love Me, Love Me, Love

1993 ***Christmas with Frank Mills***

Joy to the World • The First Noel • Good King Wenceslas • It Came Upon the Midnight Clear • We Three Kings • Silent Night • Hark the Herald Angels Sing • O Little Town of Bethlehem • Angels we Have Heard on High • Oh Holy Night • God Rest ye Merry Gentlemen • O Come all ye Faithful • Silver Bells • Holly Jolly Christmas • Jingle Bells • White Christmas • Rudolph the Red Nosed Reindeer • Frosty the Snowman • Have Yourself a Merry Little Christmas • Somewhere a Child is Sleeping • Santa Claus is Coming to Town • We Wish you a Merry Christmas

1993 ***Homeward***

The Land That I Call Home (Part 1) • Fair and Tender Ladies • Skye Boat Song • Reminiscing With you • Amazing Grace • Coming Home • When you and I Were Young, Maggie • With Someone Like you • The Land That I Call Home (Part 11) • Danny Boy • The Mountains of Mourne • Mary's Song • Shenandoah • The Land That I Call Home (Part 111) • The Road to Home • Now is the Hour

1994 ***A Traditional Christmas***

Fanfare • Angels we Have Heard on High • Away in a Manger (English version) • The Holly and the Ivy • I Saw Three Ships • The Huron Carol • Deck the Halls • Go Tell it on The Mountain • Once in Royal David's City • Away in the Manger (American version) • While Shepherds Watched Their Flocks • Mary's Boy Child • Somewhere a Child is Sleeping • When a Child is Born • Flat Baroque (After Christmas)

1996 ***Frank Mills, 25 Years of Piano Music***

Memories (from Cats) • Brahms Lullaby • I Will Always Love you • Amazing Grace • Country Piper • I Wish I Weren't Alone • Smoke Gets in Your Eyes • Ballad on a C Scale • After you Mr. Trumpet Man • Mama Won't you Boogie with me • Flat Baroque • The Land I Call Home • A Children's Song • Peter Piper • When you and I were Young • Lake Como • Seascapes • The Three Bells • Ballet Russe • Chariots of Fire • The Poet and I • The Rose • Mountains of Mourne • The Road to Home • Music Box Dancer

1996 ***Goodnight my Love***

Brahms Lullaby • Twinkle Twinkle • Fur Elise • French Child's Song • Sur le pont • Au Claire de la Lune • Waltz in A-Flat • Goodnight my Love • In May • Hush Little Baby • Whispering Hope • Pretty Horses • Mary Had/Yes Jesus

1997 ***Frank Mills goes to the Movies***

Beauty and the Beast • Rainman • Streets of Philadelphia • Terms of Endearment • Send in the Clowns • Theme from Moulin Rouge • Theme from the Silver Broom • Smile • I Will Always Love you • Smoke Gets in your Eyes • Chariots of Fire • The Rose • I Can't Help Falling in Love with you • Jurassic Park • When I Fall in Love

1997 ***Frank Mills Canada***

Farewell to Nova Scotia • Red River Valley • I'se the B'y/Alouette (medley) • Peter Amberly • Four Strong Winds • Jack was Every Inch a Sailor/Donkey Riding • Canadian Sunset • Tillsonburg Ode to Newfoundland • Squid Jiggin' Grounds • Blue Canadian Rockies • If you Could Read my Mind • The French Song • O Canada

Television Specials

1982 *Frank Mills' Christmas Special*, CTV.

1984 *Rocky Mountain Christmas with Frank Mills*, CBC.

1986 *Harvest Moon, Frank Mills' Thanksgiving Special*, CBC.

1988 *Frank Mills Christmas Concert*, CTV.

1989 *Concert in the Meadows*, Stowe, Vermont, CFCF.

1992 *An Evening with Frank Mills*, Halifax, ATV.

1994 *Christmas with Frank Mills*, Halifax, ATV/ASN.

'Music Box Dancer' facts:

* The song has sold over seven million copies.
* Sheet music sales over two million copies.
* In 1984 it earned the Million-Airs Award from Broadcast Music Inc. (BMI) for over one million radio plays in the USA.
* It became a hit in spring of 1978. By Christmas 1978, it charted in Europe and Asia, then the following April in USA. It reached Number 1 on the pop chart, and the top 40 country chart, exactly one year after starting its momentous climb.
* In March 1974, he completed his tinkly piano piece in C *sharp*. The financial picture was worsening. Previous albums weren't selling. Royalties were dribbles. The bank account was nearly empty. The hits were fading. Guy Bertrand had left Polydor to start his own company, Sonogram Records. With borrowed money, Frank recorded *Frank Mills An Instrumental Album*, with Sonogram. His untitled tinkly piano piece was the 11th cut on the album. Days before the album was recorded, seven-year-old Nancy asked her Dad to fix her battered, well-used music box. "It was a black box, ragged and beaten up from playing it so much. There was a Chinese-looking design on the outside. When you opened it there was a plastic ballerina. She had a broken arm. Cheezy rings and stuff sat on the red velvet. I asked Dad if he could fix it because she wasn't turning," remembers Nancy. When Frank looked at the ballerina with the broken arm he said, "That's it, the name of the song, 'Music Box Dancer.' " Sonogram went bankrupt about six months later. Four years later 'Music Box Dancer' became an accidential success, shortly after Frank was scheduled to start his shift as a cab driver for Beck's Cabs in Toronto.
* 'Music Box Dancer' has been recorded by such well-known pianists as Floyd Cramer and Eric Robertson, orchestrally by James Last and 101 Strings. A calypso rhythm by Germany's Roberto Delgado, a vocal version by Ray Conniff singers, and in Sweden on accordion.
* In Japan it became number one three times within one year: first Frank's original instrumental, later in Japanese, and thirdly in Chinese.
* 'Music Box Dancer' is played at the Great Wall of China.
* 'Music Box Dancer' was originally written in the key of C *sharp*, a difficult key of all black notes. Frank learned to play in the key from listening to records played at the wrong speed. Before the sheet music of 'Music Box Dancer' was produced it was changed to the key of C so it was easier to play.

Platinum Records

* 'Music Box Dancer' (single) Canada 1979
* *The Poet and I* (album) Canada 1979
* *The Poet and I* (album) Australia 1979
* *Prelude to Romance* (album) Canada 1982
* *Sunday Morning Suite* (album) Canada 1980
* *A Special Christmas* (album) Canada 1983

Gold Records

* *El Poeta Y Yo* (The Poet and I) (album) Mexico 1979
* *Frank Mills Album* (album) Canada 1981
* 'Love Me, Love Me, Love' (single) Canada 1972
* 'Music Box Dancer' (single) USA 1979
* *Music Box Dancer* (album) USA 1979
* *Rondo* (album) Canada 1982

Awards & Achievements

1976	New York Film Festival Award, "Ski East" Sound Track, U.S. A.
1979	RPM Programmers Award Top Group - Frank Mills Orchestra, Canada
1979	Instrumental Artist of the Year, Japan
1979	Top Instrumentalist, Albums (*Cash Box*) U.S.A.
1979	Top Instrumentalist, Singles (*Cash Box*) U.S.A.
1979	Top New Instrumentalist (*Record World*) U.S.A.
1980	Best Instrumental (*Record World*) U.S.A.
1980	Instrumental of the Year, Juno Award, Canada
1980	Composer of the Year, Juno Award, Canada
1980	Best Pop Instrumental Performance, Grammy Nomination. U.S.A.
1981	Instrumentalist of the Year, Juno Award, Canada
1981	Composer of the Year. William Harold Moon Award (Canada)
1983	Million-Airs Award. B.M.I. (U.S.A.)
1985	Top Musical Variety TV Show Nomination (*Rocky Mountain Christmas*) Canada

BIBLIOGRAPHY

Baskerville, David. Ph.D., *Music Business Handbook and Career Guide.* SAGE Publications, 1995.

Boden, Margaret. *The Creative Mind.* London: Cardinal Books, 1990.

Bono, Edward. *Serious Creativity; Using the Power of Lateral Thinking to Create New Ideas.* Harper Collins, 1992.

Booth, Allen. *Canadian Pop Music: 1950-1980.* Toronto: Mead Educational Ltd., 1987.

Burgess, Thornton. *Mother West Wind's Children.* Toronto: Little Brown and Company, 1911.

Byron, Lord. *The Complete Poetical Works*, p. 78. 'Childe Harold's Pilgrimage' canto III, verse 6, lines 46-54.

Byron's Letters and Journals. 12 vols., ed. Leslie A Marchand (London: John Murray, 1973-1982) vol. 3, pg. 119.

Cameron, Julia. *The Artist's Way; A Spiritual Path to Higher Creativity.* New York, NY: Jeremy P. Tarcher/Putnam Books, 1992.

Cline, Eileen. 'The Nature of Talent.' *American Suzuki Journal* Fall, 1994.

Collins, Maynard. *Lightfoot; If you Could Read his Mind.* Toronto: Deneau Publishers, 1988.

Collins, Robert. *You Had to Be There.* Toronto: McClelland & Stewart Inc, 1997.

Collinson, Francis. *The Bagpipe; The History of a Musical Instrument.* London and Boston: Routledge & Kegan Paul, 1975.

Csikszentmihalyi, Mihaly. *Creativity; Flow and the Psychology of Discovery and Invention.* New York: Harper Collins Publishers, 1996.

Dunphy, Cathy. 'Oh, you beautiful doll!' *TV Guide* December 15, 1992.

Dupuch, Etienne Jr. *Bahamas Handbook.* Nassau, Bahamas: Etienne Dupuch Jr. Publications Ltd., 1997.

Ferguson, Carol and Fraser, Margaret. *A Century of Canadian Home Cooking.* Toronto: Prentice Hall, 1992.

Gardner, Howard Dr. *Frames of Mind; The Theory of Multiple Intelligences.* New York: Basic Books, second edition, 1993.

Gitlin, Todd. *The Sixties; Years of Hope, Days of Rage.* New York: Bantam Books, 1987.

Goddard, Peter. 'Canadian clobbers musical competition.' *Toronto Star* May 5, 1979.

Hunt, Dennis. 'Frank Mills: Man with a Music Box,' *Los Angeles Times* Sunday, April 29, 1979.

Karlin, Fred. *Listening to Movies; The Film Lover's Guide to Film Music.* New York: Schirmer Books, 1994.

Kazantzakis, Nikos. *Zorba the Greek.* New York: Simon and Schuster, 1952.

Lawrence, James M and Martin, Rux. *Sweet Maple; Life, Lore and Recipes From the Sugarbush. Vermont Life*, Montpellier, Vermont and Chapters Publishing Ltd, Shelburne, Vermont. 1993.

Linden, J.J. 'Frank Mills, a four-year smash success.' *RPM* December 23, 1978.

McGee, David and Taylor, Barry. New York, NY *Record World* April 28, 1979.

Melhuish, Martin. *Heart of Gold; 30 Years of Canadian Pop Music.* Toronto: Insight Productions Company Limited, 1993.

—-. *Oh What A Feeling; A Vital History of Canadian Music.* Quarry Press, 1996.

O'Rear, John and Frankie. *The Mont Tremblant Story.* Mont Tremblant: Les Editions Altitude, 1988.

O'Neil, Thomas. *The Grammys; For The Record.* Penguin Books, 1993.

Owram, Doug. *Born at the Right Time; A History of the Baby Boom Generation.* Toronto: University of Toronto Press, 1996.

Piggott, Patrick. *The Great Composers; Rachmaninov.* London: Faber and Faber Ltd., 1978.

Perrin, Noel. *Amateur Sugar Maker.* Hanover, New Hampshire: University Press of New England, 1986.

Phillips, Jan. *Marry Your Muse; Making a Lasting Commitment to Your Creativity.* Wheaton, Illinois: Quest Books, 1997.

Porter, Darwin and Prince, Danforth. *Frommer's '98 Bahamas.* New York, NY: Simon and Schuster, 1998

Randolph, David. *This is Music; A Guide to the Pleasures of Listening.* New York: McGraw-Hill Book Company, 1964.

Ray, Charles and Ritz, David. *Brother Ray.* New York: Dial Press, 1978.

Retson, Don. 'Frank Mills hit with $10,000,000 copyright infringement suit.' *News & Chronicle* November 9, 1983.

Rutherford, Mrs. Dolly. *Rachmaninoff's Recollections Told to Oskar von Riesemann.* Translated from the German Manuscript. Freeport, New York: Books for Libraries Press, 1934.

Sloboda, John. 'What Makes a Musician?' *American Suzuki Journal* Spring, 1995.

Stone, Irving. *The Agony and the Ecstasy; A Novel of Michelangelo.* Garden City NY: Doubleday, 1961.

Storr, Anthony. *The Dynamics of Creation.* New York: Ballantine Books, 1993.

Tennyson, Alfred Lord. *Ulysses.*

Walker, Robert. *Rachmaninoff; His Life and Times.* Neptune City, NJ: Paganiniana Publications Inc., 1981.

Webb, Jimmy. 'Dancing Girl,' performed by Richard Harris on the album *A Tramp Shining.*

Wise, Carmen. 'Musical Intelligence.' *American Suzuki Journal* Fall, 1995.

Wouk, Herman. *Don't Stop the Carnival.* Garden City, New York: Doubleday & Company Inc., 1965.

Zollo, Paul. *Songwriters on Songwriting.* Cincinnati, Ohio: Writer's Digest Books, 1991.

OTHER SOURCES

Lyrics to 'Love Me, Love Me, Love.' Copyright 1971 North Country Music Ltd. Copyright assigned 1979 to Peter Piper Music Ltd. International Copyright Secured. All rights reserved. Used by permission.

News & Chronicle. 'Frank Mills: melodies his stock in trade.' Thursday, March 23, 1972.

SOCAN facts: A guide for Composers, Lyricists, Songwriters and Music Publishers. Society of Composers, Authors and Music Publishers of Canada. 1998.

Music Directory Canada. 6th edition, Norris-Whitney Communications Inc., St. Catharines, ON. 1993.

Virtual Vermont. Internet Site, September 1997.

Program Brochure, McGill Faculty of Music. Montreal, 1994.

Chart listings in:

Cash Box. December 29, 1979.

Cash Box. March 17, 1979.

US. May 15, 1979.

Billboard. March 17, 1979.

Billboard. December 8, 1979.

INDEX